50 Ways to Love Your Parents

Approaching the Heart with a Rational Mind

Sarah Cline, Ph.D.

Copyright © 2023 Sarah Cline, Ph.D.

All rights reserved.

The contents of this book may not be reproduced, duplicated, or transmitted without direct written permission from the author.

Under no circumstances will any legal responsibility or blame be held against the publisher for any reparation, damages, or monetary loss due to the information herein, either directly or indirectly.

Legal Notice:

This book is copyright-protected. This is only for personal use. You cannot amend, distribute, sell, use, quote, or paraphrase any part of the content within this book without the consent of the author.

Disclaimer Notice:

Please note the information contained within this document is for educational and entertainment purposes only. Every attempt has been made to provide accurate, up-to-date, and reliable complete information. No warranties of any kind are expressed or implied. Readers acknowledge that the author is not engaging in the rendering of legal, financial, medical, or professional advice. The content of this book has been derived from various sources. Please consult a licensed professional before attempting any techniques outlined in this book.

By reading this document, the reader agrees that under no circumstances is the author responsible for any losses, direct or indirect, which are incurred as a result of the use of the information contained within this document, including, but not limited to, errors, omissions, or inaccuracies.

ISBN: 978-1-937209-16-2

Contents

Introduction 1

1. Understanding Personality Types: A Deep Dive 4
   Origins of Personality Types
   The Introvert and the Extrovert
   Cave Dweller (CD) and Mountain Yeller (MY)
   So, How Do You Find Common Ground?
   Key Takeaways

2. Communication Is Key 19
   Express Feelings without Instigating Conflicts
   Demonstrate Active Listening Every Day
   Use Neutral Language to Curb Defensiveness
   Understand That the Dynamic is Shifting
   Understand and Respect New Boundaries as Transitions Occur
   Deal with Unresolved Childhood Issues Respectfully
   Check in with Them Often
   Schedule Personal Time for Reflection and Understanding
   Share Personal Growth Moments Regularly
   Respect Their Space and Yours
   Key Takeaways

3. Emotional Closeness 36
    Talk to Your Parents
    Don't Wait for Your Parents to Take the Lead
    Offer Surprise Gestures
    Organize Family Get-Togethers
    Walk Down Memory Lane
    Make New Memories
    Delve into Mutual Hobbies
    Bring Them Thoughtful Gifts
    Offer to Help Them
    Key Takeaways

4. Celebrate Good Times 58
    Invite Your Parents Over for Dinner
    Host Mutual Social Events or Gatherings
    Celebrate Important Holidays or Anniversaries Together
    Create Memory Gifts
    Celebrate Them "Just Because"
    Thank Them for Doing Their Best
    Recognize Their Achievements and Yours—Together
    Tell Your Parents You Love Them
    Share Life-Altering Moments with Them (Even the Bad Ones)
    Key Takeaways

5. Appreciate Them for Who They Are 68
    Celebrate Their Emotional Strengths
    Understand That They're Human—Just Like You
    Ask Them About Their Past
    Ask Them About Their Future
    Become Their Friend

    Key Takeaways

6. Boundaries and Opinions   82
    Set Boundaries for Your Parents During Major Transitions
    Ask for Advice and Listen When They Give It
    Give Them the Benefit of the Doubt During Misunderstandings
    Avoid Being Offensive with Your Language
    Don't Forget "You" Time
    Key Takeaways

7. Socializing with your Parents as an Adult   94
    Call Them Often
    Let Them Confide in You
    Hug Your Parents When You See Them
    Get Together for the Holidays
    Let Them Spend Time with Your Kids
    Treat Them
    Experience New Activities or Hobbies Together
    Take Them on Family Vacations
    Plan Family Game Nights
    Revisit Places of Significance
    Key Takeaways

8. Final Thoughts   114
    The Importance of Continuous Effort and Growth in Relationships
    Embracing the Nature of Love and Understanding

Introduction

Welcome to *50 Ways to Love Your Parents*. If you've picked up this book, you are most likely an adult or nearing an adult and eager to enhance your relationship with your parents. By reading this, you have taken a significant step toward deeper understanding and connection—so, congratulations are in order.

Throughout this volume and larger series, we'll focus on three universal personality categories: the reserved Cave Dweller (CD), the outgoing Mountain Yeller (MY), and the Straddler, who exhibits mixed traits. Recognizing and understanding these types is crucial, as they shape relationship dynamics in untold ways. Our aim is to provide practical insights into fundamental personalities, ensuring you're better equipped to navigate and strengthen your relationships. What's more, you'll walk away with a better grasp of who *you* truly are—and by knowing yourself, you're better for others.

Armed with the insights from this book, you'll not only interpret actions but also understand the deeper motivations behind them with greater ease. Prepare to see your parents—and perhaps yourself—in a whole new light...

The Power of Personalities

Ahead, we'll demystify the core attributes of CDs, MYs, and Straddlers, equipping you with insights to comprehend and appreciate the nuances of each type. Appreciating these differences allows you to interpret your parent's behaviors accurately within their unique personality contexts, thus avoiding flawed assumptions.

Too often in relationships, we mistakenly attribute conflicts and misunderstandings to a lack of love, empathy, or respect. Yet, more frequently, it's a simple gap in understanding. When we don't perceive the underlying personality traits driving our parents' actions, we can misinterpret their intentions, leading to undue tension. It's not always about agreeing or having the same viewpoint; it's about acknowledging and respecting these inherent differences. By recognizing the core personality traits of CDs, MYs, and Straddlers, we can better empathize with our parents, allowing love to fully flourish.

Before We Begin

50 Ways to Love Your Parents offers no quick fix or casual checklist. Instead, it emphasizes "love" as an active endeavor, demanding both attention and effort. While you'll find a great deal of guidance here, it's up to you to apply these insights authentically.

Engaging with this material will require introspection, and there will be moments that challenge your current understanding of parenting and relationships—and everything else for that matter. Yet, it's in these times of reflection and adjustment that true growth happens…and, here, the fruits of your labor could scarcely be sweeter—some real incentive.

Through patience and ongoing application, you're not just enhancing a single bond but, rather, refining how you connect. How you live. How you share your soul. So, love the process, love yourself, and love your parents on a whole new level.

Before we begin, remind yourself: you're a masterpiece—and a work in progress, as is your relationship with your parents.

Chapter One

Understanding Personality Types: A Deep Dive

Do you find yourself needing help understanding your parents' personality traits? Are you frustrated that they're so dissimilar to yours?

Understanding personality types is an essential piece of the puzzle when seeking to understand your parents. Appreciating them means discovering their true layers and complexities, and all of them should garner your attention if you are ever to experience a happy and healthy relationship.

In this chapter, we will discuss the personality types of the Cave Dweller parent, which we will refer to as CD, the Mountain Yeller parent or MY, and the Straddler parent. Learning about these three basic personality types will give you a clearer picture of the unique benefits and challenges each creates. And understanding is an essential first step to bringing harmony and happiness into your everyday life.

Origins of Personality Types

Before the modern-day classifications of CDs and MYs and even before psychiatrists and psychologists stepped onto the scene, ancient civilizations sought to explain human behavior and its various nuances.

The Ancient Greeks

The ancient Greeks developed the theory of "four humors" to explain the causes of health and illness, both mental and physical. This theory suggested that an individual's temperament was influenced by bodily fluids: blood (sanguine), yellow bile (choleric), black bile (melancholic), and phlegm (phlegmatic). The Greeks thought these humors were directly related to being sanguine (cheerful), choleric (short-tempered), melancholic (reserved), or phlegmatic (relaxed). Therefore, the balance of these humors was believed to influence an individual's temperament, health, and overall disposition. An imbalance in these humors led to behaviors that, today, we associate with certain mental illnesses. For example:

- Sanguine (blood) was associated with cheerful, optimistic, enthusiastic personality traits. An imbalance was thought to be due to a person having too much blood in their body, which would cause them to be overly confident and have impulsive behavior. Possible narcissistic and bipolar disorder.

- Choleric (yellow bile) was associated with being ambitious, passionate, and easily angered. An imbalance causes anger, irritability, or extremely aggressive behavior and rage. Possible borderline personality disorder.

- Melancholic (black bile) was associated with being thoughtful, reflective, and often sad or depressed. This imbalance was associated with melancholy and depression.

- Phlegmatic (phlegm) was associated with being calm, reliable, and often unemotional or apathetic. An imbalance was associated with lethargy, sluggishness, or a lack of motivation, which, much like melancholic, is a symptom of depression.

Treating these emotional ailments is where things got even more interesting. If the Greeks thought you had an imbalance of any of these four humors, you would likely have received one of the following treatments:

- **Dietary Changes:** Prescribed depending on the humor in excess. For instance, someone deemed overly choleric might be advised to avoid hot or spicy foods that would "agitate" the yellow bile.

- **Bloodletting:** If you were someone believed to have an excess of sanguine humor, it was common practice to be prescribed bloodletting. This process involved removing blood from the body by way of leeches or actual cutting.

- **Purging:** To remove excess bile or phlegm, laxatives were used, as were emetics, which induced vomiting.

- **Baths/Sweating:** To promote toxin removal, balms and ointments were applied to the skin to help imbalance these four humors.

The Greeks' attempts to "treat" imbalances in personality or health were based on the observations and the knowledge they had at the time. The four humors theory was eventually replaced with more accurate medical models, but its influence can still be seen in some of our languages today.

The Introvert and the Extrovert

Carl Gustav Jung (1875–1961) was a Swiss psychiatrist, psychoanalyst, and the father of analytical psychology. He developed several concepts that had a profound influence on both psychology and popular culture. One of his most notable contributions was the concept of "introversion" and "extraversion" (often used in the more modern manner: introvert and extrovert). Jung's theory asserts that introversion and extraversion are attitudes that represent the direction in which a person's psychic energy flows.

Extraversion (Extrovert)

According to Jung, the extrovert's energy flows outward. This personality type is more oriented toward the external world and derives energy from interacting with its surroundings, including people, events, and situations. If your parent is an extrovert, they tend to be more outgoing, social, and interested in external events. They are typically action-oriented and more comfortable in social situations than an introverted parent. External factors influence parental extroverts, who are occasionally prone to negative introspection.

Introversion (Introvert)

As the name suggests, the introvert's energy flows inward. This personality type is more oriented toward the internal world, relying on introspection and internal reflection. If your parent is introverted, they are generally more reserved and often feel more comfortable with individual activities or smaller group settings. They derive energy and pleasure from thinking, daydreaming, or exploring ideas. Although an introverted person's daily practices tend to lead to social isolation, they tend to have a small number of deep connections with people of their choosing.

Jung believed that everyone has an introverted and extroverted side, with one being more dominant than the other. It's a spectrum, and while some people might be near the extremes of that spectrum, most individuals lie somewhere in between.

Cave Dweller (CD) and Mountain Yeller (MY)

While not strictly rooted in these historical contexts, the CD and MY classifications are evolved constructs reflecting the same human desire to understand ourselves and others in our world more deeply.

While our contemporary understanding of the CD and MY classifications doesn't stem directly from ancient Greek or Jungian theories, much like their historical counterparts, they are observed patterns in modern relationships. By identifying recurring patterns, we can forge tools to help us navigate and harmonize interpersonal interactions.

Deeper Dive into the Cave Dweller (CD)

We must first learn about their traits to determine whether you and your parents fall into the CD or MY category.

Reserved Nature

If your parent is a CD, they will predominantly be calm and reserved. CDs are introspective and tend to hold their emotions close to their chest because they value their inner world and the sanctuary it provides. Their reserved nature doesn't mean that they are indifferent or don't care about those around them; it just means that they process their emotions internally and over time.

For instance, after an argument, a CD might withdraw to process their feelings rather than immediately confront an issue. A CD does this because they typically feel uncomfortable with strife and need time to work through their emotions and how to communicate their feelings.

Socially, a CD is often found in quieter corners, engaging in deep conversation with one or two individuals rather than in the center of a party. In group discussions, a CD will offer insights only if specifically asked or if they feel strongly about a topic.

Logical Thinking and Literal Communication

A CD leans more toward analytical and logical thinking. They make decisions only after careful contemplation and weighing the pros and cons. They work hard to keep their emotions from clouding their judgment. This logical thinking manifests in their communication; they will get to the point without inserting emotions or using stories to embellish their point.

For example, if you discuss a film with a CD, they will likely dissect plot points with impeccable logic and even point out strengths and weaknesses. But they often miss the emotional undertones of the movie. If you ask a CD if they liked the cake you brought for dessert, they might reply, "Yes," without diving into flowery descriptives.

It's important to note that a CD may also get frustrated with an embellished story that takes longer to get to the point. It doesn't mean they don't want to hear the story or don't care what you have to say; their brain is just geared toward immediate outcomes.

Need for Space

A CD has an inherent need for emotional and physical personal space. For them, requiring space is not about distancing themselves from loved ones. It's about needing solitude to recharge and reflect.

CDs enjoy reading books in a cozy nook or going for solitary walks. They may listen to music while cooking dinner instead of talking. This alone time is essential for a CD, especially after a day filled with social interactions.

Singular Focus

A CD has unparalleled concentration when engrossed in a task and prefers completing that task to their satisfaction before tackling another.

If you attempt to talk to a CD while they're writing an email, for example, they may be so absorbed in what they're writing that you'll be tuned out. It's not that what you're saying is unimportant to them; it's just challenging for them to spread their focus on more than one thing at a time because they give each item their full attention.

Social Preferences

Traditionally, if your parent is labeled an introvert, others would consider them anti-social. But that couldn't be farther from the truth. An introvert, or a CD, just leans toward more intimate social interactions. Large gatherings can overwhelm a CD and drain their mental and emotional battery.

Emotional Processing

While CDs might not outwardly express their emotions, they experience them deeply. However, their internal reflections may lead to a delay in their outward emotional expression. While a CD may seem distant after an emotional confrontation, they must process the interaction before reacting. A CD needs time to contemplate a disagreement, analyze the conversation, and figure out where things went wrong before they can move on to a resolution. This meditation is essential for a CD's family member to understand; the more you push them to express themselves, the more they will clam up in response.

Deeper Dive into the Mountain Yeller (MY)

If your parent is an extrovert, chances are they've been called that more than once in their lifetime. An extrovert is typically known for being outgoing and the life of any party. But there's so much more to them than meets the eye.

Outgoing Nature/Group Socialization

An MY is inherently outgoing. Their energy thrives on interactions and being around people as often as possible. Instead of needing time alone to recharge, MYs wants to be out and involved.

At a social event, MYs will be the first to initiate games and dancing and will often bounce from person to person, catching up rather than focusing on one task at a time. Deep conversations are still on the table, but not at a social event. An MY usually rallies their friends for a group outing over a weekend rather than sitting at home reading a book or watching TV. Even in the workplace, MYs love group projects and find collaborative brainstorming and teamwork exciting.

Emotion-Driven

MYs are heart-ruled because they lead with their intuition and emotions. Being ruled by their heart doesn't mean their decisions are devoid of logic, but their feelings heavily influence their reactions. MYs can be emotional during arguments but are also the first to send a heartfelt message to a friend or family member upon hearing they are having a rough time.

An MY's emotions will show throughout their storytelling, so be patient when they tell you about an event or relay the plot to a movie. Chances are both will be full of details and embellishments.

Connection and Touch

MYs crave genuine connections and physical touch. Whether it's a hug, a pat on the back, or simply holding hands. It reinforces their feeling of being connected. In relating with you, an MY will crave physical affection and see it as a top priority over other needs—something we'll discuss in depth a bit later.

Dynamic Focus

An MY is a natural multitasker. Instead of focusing on one task at a time, their attention shifts between assignments. They enjoy the energy they get from juggling multiple things and often get bored working on one project for an extended period.

An MY doesn't mind dealing with paperwork but works through it while watching television or listening to music. As for conversations, an MY loves to chat, but don't be surprised if you find them scrolling on their phone while talking with you. It's not that they think what you have to say is unimportant; their mind simply runs at a faster rate than a CD's, making them more comfortable processing more than one thing at a time.

Inferential Communication

An MY often communicates using stories, anecdotes, and metaphors rather than getting straight to the point. They rely on indirect implications and expect others to infer meanings, which can confuse some who aren't familiar with their communication style.

During an argument, someone may find it hard to decipher what the MY really wants, even if they feel they have told them directly. It's essential to have a middle ground where communication is concerned, especially if your parent is an MY and you are a CD. Because the communication styles between personalities are very different.

Immediate Emotional Expression

Unlike their CD counterparts, MYs are quick to express their emotions. They're an open book and rarely hesitate to share their feelings of joy and disappointment. This can be overwhelming for a CD uncomfortable with an emotional display.

One of the greatest fears an MY faces is the fear of rejection. If an MY has a CD child who usually pulls away at any sign of conflict, this can be a bone of contention. An MY will take a CD child's withdrawal as a sign of personal rejection. If you are a CD with an MY parent, it's important to communicate that you are not rejecting them and need time to wrap your head around and process the disagreement. Give the MY verbal and physical affirmations whenever possible.

If you are a CD and your parent is an MY, don't panic; it doesn't mean you cannot have a successful parent/child relationship. There are plenty of amazing and fulfilling relationships between opposites. It just means it will take time, work, and patience to learn one another's needs and effectively communicate.

The Straddler

If your parent is a Straddler, they are adaptable and enjoy the best of both worlds. They can immerse themselves in a book like a CD or be the life of a party like an MY. They possess an emotional agility that allows them to straddle their personality types seamlessly. While this book predominantly focuses on CD and MY personality types, Straddlers can use it to understand the extremes and navigate their middle ground more effectively.

Excellent Balance between Reflection and Expression

A Straddler can introspect like a CD, valuing quiet moments of thought. Yet, they also appreciate the expressive vitality that an MY has and share their feelings and ideas openly when a situation calls for it. They are as happy spending a quiet evening reading and attending a book club as they are actively participating in a lively discussion.

Adaptable in Social Situations

While they might not always be the life of the party, they easily adjust to situations based on the social settings and the company involved.

They can engage in a one-on-one conversation at a party and then join a group game or be at the party's center later in the evening.

Values: Both Logic and Emotion

A Straddler approaches situations with a logical mindset but is equally attuned to the emotional undercurrents, valuing the importance of feelings in decision-making. For example, if a colleague faces a personal issue, the Straddler will offer practical solutions while providing emotional support.

Flexibility in Needs and Fears

The Straddler's hierarchy of needs will fluctuate based on circumstances, and they might experience the same fears from a CD's spectrum, such as loss of security, as well as the MY's fear of rejection. However, adaptability allows them to prioritize different aspects of their life. While working on an important business project, they will prioritize career stability, but in downtime, they will focus on relationships and personal connections.

Fluid Communication Styles

A Straddler can communicate directly and inferentially, often adjusting communication based on the recipient. For example, when conversing with an analytical boss, they will be direct and to the point, but when they talk to their best friend, they become expressive and delve into all the nitty-gritty details.

Straddlers possess an innate ability to mediate and find common ground, especially in relationships where CDs and MYs might find themselves at odds. Their adaptability enables them to comprehend and empathize with both personality types, easing communication and diminishing misunderstandings.

A Straddler may seem like the perfect personality type. However, everyone encounters their share of struggles. The flexibility of a Straddler often confuses their preferences and needs. The Straddler might sometimes feel stretched or trapped in the middle, particularly in a polarized situation where they wish to please others so much that they struggle to voice their disagreements. A Straddler must discern what is truly significant to them while learning to navigate others' personality types, much like everyone else.

So, How Do You Find Common Ground?

"I'm a CD, and my parent is an MY; is my relationship with them doomed?"

No! In this book, we don't tell you how to "cope" with differences. We allow you to realize each person's unique strengths in a relationship. A CD's introspection can balance an MY's spontaneity. An MY's vivacity and exuberance can harmonize beautifully with a CD's depth and stability.

Recognizing these different traits is merely the first step to a healthy relationship. The real challenge, and indeed the focus of this book, is to find ways to navigate the complexities of these interactions. After all, the beauty of a relationship truly unfolds in the dance between these personalities.

Key Takeaways

Diving into the intricacies of personality types isn't about affixing labels but enriching our understanding. With these insights, you're now armed with the necessary vocabulary to navigate the labyrinth of human emotions and connections, fostering an environment where love thrives, understanding blossoms, and relationships flourish. As we traverse this journey, let's remember that the goal isn't to change but to adapt, understand, and love more deeply.

The foundation for a nurturing relationship starts with understanding—understanding yourself, your parents, and the dynamics of your interaction. With the knowledge of CD and MY personality traits, you're well on your way to deepening that understanding, setting the stage for the subsequent chapters that will guide you on how to cherish your parents in ways that resonate with all of you.

Understanding personality differences is essential for nurturing compatibility. This chapter has illuminated the fundamental traits of CDs, MYs, and Straddlers.

- **Reserved Nature:** Respect your CD parents' need for personal space and quiet reflection. Don't force immediate emotional reactions.

- **Logical Thinking:** Recognize your CD parents' analytical approach. Be patient as they process before expressing feelings.

- **Singular Focus:** Acknowledge that multitasking is difficult for your CD parent. Allow them to complete or pause their task before they give you their full attention.

- **Emotion-Driven:** Empathize with your MY parents' emotions. Give them positive affirmations/compliments and physical affection.

- **Inferential Communication:** Listen for meanings implied indirectly in your MY parents' stories. Learn to read between the lines.

- **Dynamic Focus:** Accept your MY parents' wandering attention. Multitasking is in their nature. However, if you need their full focus, tell them.

- **Excellent Balance:** Appreciate the adaptability of a Straddler but avoid putting them in the middle of conflicts.

- **Flexible Needs:** Accommodate shifts in a Straddler's priorities. Reassure them of your unconditional love.

Chapter Two

Communication Is Key

Effective communication is the foundation of any healthy relationship, regardless of whether it is a romantic relationship or a parent/child relationship. It also does not discriminate against personality type.

Communication is the bridge that connects us all—whether we are CDs or Mys. It enables us to come to a mutual understanding and build a stronger bond.

In this chapter, we'll delve into the essential components of communication that can strengthen the bond you have with both of your parents. Moreover, the chapter will navigate the traits of each personality type and how you can use personality indicators to validate your parents, yourself, and all of your needs.

While it's easy to be swayed by the idea that love is a mysterious force beyond our control, the reality is that maintaining a lasting relationship requires a lot more than just love. It requires conscious effort, respect, and a willingness to understand one another on a deeper level. This journey of appreciation goes beyond knowing your parents' favorite "things" or doing what you think will make them "happy". It's about diving deep into their psyche, comprehending their unique personality traits, and recognizing how their attributes interact with yours.

In the digital connections and instant gratification age, we sometimes forget the beauty of human interaction. We often overlook the importance of patience, reflection, and presence with our loved ones. Thus, you can pause, reflect, and feel as we progress through this chapter. By fostering an environment of open communication and mutual respect, you're not just building relationships and bonds but cultivating relationships that thrive on understanding, compassion, and genuine connection. Here are some strategies and ground rules to help you convey your emotions effectively:

Express Feelings without Instigating Conflicts

Expressing your feelings is crucial for any relationship, but it's also essential to do so without triggering conflicts. It's too easy to get wrapped up in emotions when expressing them to someone else—especially when you're first sorting through them—so it's crucial to take a step back, breathe, and formulate thoughts before verbalizing them. This is especially true with your parents. Sometimes tensions are high; and as an adult, you may think it is your opportunity to lay everything out on the table. While this can be true—and even beneficial—it is important to understand how to do it healthily. Make sure to keep the heightened emotions to a minimum to avoid as much conflict as possible.

Remain Calm

Try not to overreact to difficult situations. By remaining calm, it's more likely that your parents will respect you enough to see your perspective.

Express Feelings with Words, Not Actions

If you start to get angry and feel you may lose control, take a break, and do something to help yourself feel calm.

- Take a walk.
- Do breathing exercises.
- Interact with a pet.
- Journal
- Read a book.

Address One Issue at a Time

Only introduce tertiary issues once the primary problem has been fully discussed. This way, you'll avoid what experts call the "kitchen sink effect". Dr. John Mordechai Gottman (born April 26, 1942), an American psychologist and professor at the University of Washington, coined the term to describe the act of one person in a discussion or argument throwing "everything but the kitchen sink" into it by dredging up past mistakes and grievances. This tactic is particularly counterproductive, as it's often overwhelming to the person receiving the grievances. This is especially true of your parents. Even if you have childhood grievances, avoid bringing them all up during a time of argument or debate. These are better suited to planned discussions. Family therapy sessions are especially helpful in these sorts of situations.

Resist Underhandedness

Avoid hitting below the belt or being underhanded. Never use these conversations to attack your parents—especially in sensitive areas. These attacks only foster distrust, anger, and harmful vulnerability. We don't want to "win" arguments, we want to work through issues by effectively communicating.

Avoid Clamming Up

Positive results can only be obtained by way of proper communication. It's easy to feel emotionally charged when discussing your feelings with your parents, especially if they've upset you or you think they're upset with you. When emotions run high, we often "clam up" or shut down.

It's important to note that when one person becomes silent and stops responding, frustration and anger can quickly follow. If you feel overwhelmed or as though you're shutting down, you may need to take a break from the discussion. Just remember to follow up on the discussion later. Likewise, respect the fact that it may be your parents who need the space.

Be Specific and Productive

Be precise about what is bothering you. Try not to generalize. Avoid words like "never" or "always." These sweeping terms are usually inaccurate anyway and will (almost) always heighten tensions. Instead of using hyperbolic, focus on what you're feeling in the moment. Vague complaints are also challenging to address, and tackling each specific item productively is important.

Demonstrate Active Listening Every Day

Practice active listening when your parents communicate with you, and avoid interrupting them when they're speaking, even if you disagree. Active listening is the cornerstone of all effective communication. It involves not only hearing the words they say but also understanding their emotions and perspectives. Validate them and show them that you're listening by maintaining eye contact and providing non-verbal cues such as nodding. Our body language matters.

Be present in the conversation and take their feelings and criticisms seriously. Don't be distracted by external forces. Never multitask while someone is communicating with you. Listen to and reflect on what they are saying before responding. Be sure to ask open-ended questions to encourage them to share more and remember one thing: if they are communicating it, it's important.

Use Neutral Language to Curb Defensiveness

Your choice of words can significantly impact the tone of your communication. To prevent defensiveness and promote understanding, avoid accusatory language, and instead focus on the specific behavior or issue. Accusations will lead your parents to focus on defending themselves rather than understanding you or your perspective. Instead, discuss how an action made you feel.

Use "We" Statements

Using "we" instead of "you" statements conveys that you are in this together and working as a team to resolve a problem. It's important to communicate that you are practicing empathy and acknowledging their feelings and perspectives.

Don't Say This:
"You never understand where I'm coming from."

Instead, Say This:
"We seem to have a disconnect sometimes in our communication."

Emphasizing "we" makes the conversation more about finding solutions together rather than pointing fingers, which can often lead to a more productive and less confrontational discussion.

Use "I" Statements

Expressing yourself without becoming overly aggressive can be challenging when faced with a conflict, especially if your parents are pushing your buttons, or have been acting out a lot recently. To help de-escalate the situation and clarify your point, an "I" or an assertive statement is an effective, psychiatrist-approved approach.

Suppose there's a conflict where you feel your parents are always getting involved with your life in ways you don't necessarily want them to be involved.

Don't Say This:
"You are always nagging me."

Instead, Say This:
"I feel a little overwhelmed when you assert your opinion or offer unsolicited advice. I would like us to set boundaries for this so we can always be on the same page."

This "I" statement expresses your feelings and needs without blaming or accusing them. After all, if you're having this conversation, it's because your parent wants to help—even when you don't want them to.

Using language that emphasizes how you feel is much more effective communication and is less likely to result in your parents shutting down or getting angry. It also aids in their ability to empathize and see things from your perspective. Here's another example:

Don't Say This:
"You never listen to me." (This is also likely a generalization.)

Instead, Say This:
"I feel frustrated when I feel unheard. I would like it if we worked on listening to each other a little more effectively."

Speaking this way avoids tactics of attack, critique, and criticism, which usually lead to more hostility and defensiveness. In general, using "I" messages can create a constructive dialogue about the true causes of any conflict by avoiding aggressive behaviors and fostering effective communication.

Understand That the Dynamic is Shifting

As we grow older, the relationship between us and our parents shifts. The dynamic changes. We are no longer infants, relying on our parents for our every need. Once we hit adolescence, we start growing more independent and obtaining more and more responsibilities—and then we become adults.

When we are younger, we just see our parents in their one particular role: our parents. We don't actually think of them as having identities beyond that. Then we grew up and realized that they actually had lives before us. In adulthood, you realize that your parents have their own identities and no longer have to take care of you—this can cause your relationship to shift.

Possibly even to...friendship?

Upon entering the unchartered waters of being an adult child, you realize that you and your parents can now get to know each other as individuals. And with that, there is a whole new dynamic to your relationship. Suddenly, you are all on an equal footing, and the more you get to know them as people—rather than just your parents—the more likely that you find that you are actually becoming friends with your parents.

Understand that you can still ask for advice but know that they may now also ask for yours. When you were younger, it is likely you never experienced your parents asking you for advice. After all, that makes sense, you weren't old enough to have any real-life experience. But now that you're older, more mature, and likely have your life together, your parents see you almost as a peer.

Understand and Respect New Boundaries as Transitions Occur

As the dynamic shifts, so should your boundaries with your parents. But what are normal boundaries to have as an adult with your parents?

These include having your own space and being seen as an adult capable of making decisions on your own. Healthy boundaries include appreciating one another and each other's time and feeling safe enough to share sensitive information. Your parents must understand that you are not a child anymore and can enforce limits as you need them. Examples of common boundaries we should set with parents include:

- Making them call you before they come over.

- Them understanding that you don't want unsolicited relationship or marriage advice.

- Respecting and avoiding comments on your life choices just because they disagree with them.

- Making them understand that as an adult, you do have other priorities.

- Giving you a physical space to be yourself and not invade your privacy.

Is It Disrespectful to Set Boundaries with Parents?

Some people may worry that setting boundaries with their parents is considered disrespectful. Boundaries set by children (even adult children) can feel disrespectful to some parents, making you feel worse for enforcing them. But it's still important to set them.

General Tips to Set Boundaries with Parents

If you are unsure where to start when setting boundaries with your parents, consider the following:

- **Know Your Limits:** Knowing your limits is the first step before setting boundaries. If you know what boundaries you will need and know your parents may violate them, it's better to be proactive than reactive. It's also better to discuss the potential consequences of violating these boundaries.

- **Let Go of Guilt Over Having Boundaries:** Guilting yourself for wanting or having boundaries is putting yourself through tough emotions twice. There is no need for that! Your needs are valid.

- **Be Direct:** Although this may be challenging, especially in young adulthood, being direct about your feelings truly can go a long way. If you tiptoe the issue, you're not helping anyone because you likely aren't being honest—and your parents ultimately cannot read your mind. They will never know it's necessary if you aren't honest and open.

- **Know When You Need Space:** Knowing when you might need a timeout is vital. If you need space or alone time, that is nothing to feel guilty over. Communicate those needs with your parents to ensure everyone is at full mental capacity and health when you come together.

Deal with Unresolved Childhood Issues Respectfully

Communicating about past issues or traumas may be necessary in order to continue your relationship with your parents, especially in a healthy way. It is important that we do this carefully and respectfully and avoid language and situations that could flare the issue.

First thing first, acknowledge and recognize the trauma or issue for what it is. If you had real trauma in your childhood, don't minimize the event or dismiss it by pretending it didn't happen. Don't succumb to feelings of guilt or self-blame. Acknowledge it for its true nature because that is the first and only way you begin to heal.

The next thing is to regain control. Feelings of helplessness can carry well over into adulthood and can make you feel and act like a victim, causing you to make choices based on your past. When you're a victim, you hold no control because you are burdened by the past. If you're seeking a relationship with your parents after something you feel is their fault that has forced you into feeling helpless or traumatized, it is always best to seek professional help in therapy. Consider family counseling for the safety and wellbeing of all of you.

However, if you feel there are issues from your childhood that you need to discuss with your parents, and you don't feel you need professional intervention, just make sure that you're communicating with them respectfully, using neutral language, and don't negate their feelings either. Remember to demonstrate active listening, respect one another, and give each other space as it's needed.

Check in with Them Often

Check-ins can be just to see how your parents are doing, or they can hold a deeper meaning. They can be great times to do reflection exercises and to truly delve into one another's wellbeing and psyche. If you have set boundaries with your parents recently, or vice versa, discuss together how everything is going.

Schedule Personal Time for Reflection and Understanding

Allocating time for personal reflection and understanding enhances self-awareness and empathy. It gives proper time for each person to discover their unique needs, as well as their strengths and weaknesses. Admitting personal faults to ourselves—let alone others—isn't easy. So, consider setting aside moments for self-reflection. Specialists also recommend you journal these thoughts to better understand your emotions and to have the ability to look back at your progress. Encourage your family members to do the same and share your insights with one another when you're ready.

Use this personal time to explore your progress and how those advancements align with your parents' journey of self-awareness. Self-awareness refers to a clear understanding of your own emotions, strengths, weaknesses, thoughts, and beliefs—and how they might influence your behavior, including your interactions with others. Being self-aware is fundamental for healthy relationships with yourself and others. Understanding ourselves means understanding our needs, expectations, boundaries, and communication styles. All of this shapes how we interact and love our family members and friends.

When we're not self-aware, we open the door to harmful interactions due to blind spots in our communication and waning emotional health. A lack of self-awareness can lead to:

- Poor emotional regulation, which results in outbursts and other unhealthy expressions of anger or hurt.

- Personal neglect and impaired mental health.

- A skewed perception of reality caused by biases and defense mechanisms that build up over time. (Also, without self-awareness, a person tends to reject constructive criticism, thus missing out on potential personal growth.)

- Communication blind spots.

- Crossing boundaries, whether they are your own boundaries or the boundaries of others.

Being more self-aware gives us the tools necessary to have satisfying and successful relationships. It just makes sense. Know yourself, and you'll have the foundation for a life and relationship that isn't just surviving but thriving.

Share Personal Growth Moments Regularly

Using feedback obtained from your scheduled meetings, emotional discussions, and self-awareness exercises, you can begin to document your personal development. Once again, journaling is a great way to record feedback and your own reflections. It can provide a glimpse of previous versions of yourself and give greater insight into your personal growth.

Personal growth is an ongoing journey and it's important to share these moments of realization—even epiphanies—with your loved ones. Discuss your personal experiences, challenges, and lessons learned through self-reflection and check-ins with your parents. Nothing feels better than knowing we've helped someone, so when your parents help you out, be sure to tell them!

Along the way, support one another's aspirations and encourage continued self-improvement exercises. Then, go on to celebrate milestones in your personal development journey together. By following these guidelines and strategies, you can improve your communication with your parents, whether they are CDs or Mys. Effective communication is the key to understanding, empathy, and building a strong and thriving relationship.

Respect Their Space and Yours

When your parents come to visit, welcome them warmly. If your parents live with you, show respect for their space; when you're in their rooms, try to make them feel like you are visiting their house. And likewise, ask them to respect your space as well. Communicate where boundaries need to be and what works best for your family.

If you don't live with your parents, communicate timeframes and expectations for visiting and going out together. Make sure you all respect your individual needs and give each other space when necessary.

Key Takeaways

Effective communication forms the foundation of all healthy and flourishing relationships. It goes beyond the confines of personality types, but learning about them can be a great place to start.

This chapter has explored how you might engage with your parents on a deeper level. Start difficult discussions by expressing feelings without instigating conflicts. It is important, no matter what happens, to remain calm and collect yourself before delving headfirst into the conversation. Remember, your parents are more likely to consider your perspective if they feel that they can voice their concerns without you jumping off the deep end or responding out of anger and vice versa.

The best ways to express yourself without conflict is to:

- **Express Feelings with Words, Not Actions:** If you feel anger rising to an uncontrollable level, take a step back and return to the conversation after you've calmed down. Consider engaging in other activities that help you regain your composure. Encourage your parents to do the same. Use methods like walking, deep breathing, or journaling to manage strong emotions constructively.

- **Address One Issue at a Time:** Avoid resorting to the "kitchen sink" approach. Focus on one issue at a time when discussing conflicts.

- **Resist Underhandedness:** Steer clear of using underhanded or hurtful tactics when discussing sensitive topics with your parents. Attacking them in sensitive areas only fosters distrust, anger, and vulnerability, which is counterproductive to communication.

- **Be Specific and Productive:** When expressing concerns, be specific and avoid making generalized statements using words like "never" or "always." Broad complaints are challenging to address and usually aren't even true.

Once all of you can communicate effectively, make sure that you are demonstrating active listening skills during conversations and that you're using neutral language. "I" and "We" statements are best to be employed to emphasize that you are working together for a common goal and not that you are attacking them.

CDs may be a little less vocal during communications, and that's okay! Appreciate the silence. Allow them the space and time to collect their thoughts and feelings. Avoid pressuring them to speak immediately after a conflict, and create a safe environment where silence is just considered a part of the communication process.

Mys on the other hand don't do as well with silence. Make sure that you are offering verbal affirmations to help them feel safe and loved during communication. Compliment them genuinely.

The next thing we learned about is how the dynamic may shift as you grow older. Recognize that the parent-child relationship evolves, and you begin to see your parents as individuals with their own lives and identities is crucial. This transition can even lead to a friendship if boundaries are respected as these transitions occur.

Remember to deal with any past or unresolved issues respectfully and check in with your parents often after important conversations or boundaries are set just to get an idea of how everyone is feeling and gauge how everyone feels it's going.

Make sure you schedule personal time for reflection and communicate your findings with your family during these check-ins; and finally, respect one another and the space that you all may need individually.

By following these guidelines and strategies, you can improve your communication with your parents, fostering understanding, empathy, and a strong, thriving relationship as you navigate the shifting dynamics of adult-child and parent relationships.

Chapter Three

Emotional Closeness

In Chapter 3 of our guide, we delve into the importance of emotional closeness between parents and their adult children. This chapter explores various aspects of building and maintaining a strong emotional connection with your parents, highlighting the value of open communication. We explore how to overcome feeling afraid to talk about certain things with our parents to really be able to open up, and the importance of understanding differing perspectives. We then move into other areas to improve the emotional bond you have with your parents and how offering surprise gestures can help show your appreciation to them.

Your parents are emotional beings and appreciate effort. This chapter delves into making them a priority and learning how to devote time and energy to making them happy and fostering the growth of your relationship.

Talk to Your Parents

Talking about your problems can help and give you much-needed catharsis or even just give you a chance to vent. In fact, regular family communication can affect your psychological well-being.

Communication with your family is important for your development, and it has been proven to have many benefits.

These benefits include:

- Identity formation
- Exploration of identity
- Moral reasoning
- Physical and psychological maturity

However, some may feel that talking with their parents is extremely difficult. This is true, initially, due to different vantage points.

Why It Can Be Difficult to Speak to Your Parents

Differing Perspectives

During adolescence, parents often don't see things the same way that their children do. Research reports that a majority of teenagers feel their families are not open, cohesive, or adaptable—and overall have problems. Whereas those same reports show that their parents have differing opinions.

It is likely that you and your parents see things differently in your family, and that this issue has transcended your childhood and seeped into adulthood. What you think is lacking, your parents may be perfectly content with. This could potentially lead to a major disconnect and make communication increasingly more difficult.

Shame or Fear

Even in a situation where you feel you might have a fairly open relationship with your parents and can freely speak to them, it can still be potentially daunting. This is generally in regard to topics or incidents that trigger feelings of shame and embarrassment.

Talking to your parents about mental health or sexuality can be particularly difficult because those subjects are typically covered in stigmas. Feeling about being judged, perceived negatively, or even misunderstood prevents people from opening up in general, so it is to be expected that it could be difficult to open up to your parents or other adults in these sorts of situations. You may not want your parents to think less of you or be disappointed. In such a situation, silence may seem easier than talking.

Sometimes, just the fear of reprimands or scolding—or even just making one's parents angry can make us afraid to talk openly to them.

Tips for talking to your parents include:

- **Defining the Intention of a Conversation Before You Have It:** If you know that it is going to be a difficult conversation, define the purpose or the outcome you're hoping for. Do you need your parents to meet a need you may have? Do you need them to clarify something? Or are you looking for them to solve a problem? Once you figure this out, the objective will be clearer to you—which in turn should make the direction of the conversation easier to navigate.

- **Preparing and Organizing Your Thoughts:** Whether you want to write things down, type them out on your phone, or practice the conversation in front of the mirror, prepare yourself before having the talk. Try to organize your thoughts so that you feel more confident during the conversation. Once this is done, determine a time and a place; and if you can, tell your parents you have something important to discuss with them and ask them when a good time would be.

- **Dispel Negative Emotions:** If you need to talk to your parents about having a difficult time—or if something is causing anxiety, make sure you let them know you're going to be speaking about something that is difficult for you. Speaking about those feelings may help reduce negative emotions on their end. By making them aware of your mental state, you may also make them take extra care to make it a comfortable space for you.

- **Try to Understand Their Perspective:** There will be many things that you and your parents don't agree on, even as you get older. Generational gaps can play a big role in this. It's important to use active listening (as discussed in Chapter 2) to truly understand them and their point of view.

- **Explain What You Need From Them:** In order for the conversation to go well, it is important to be clear about what you need from your parents. For example, do you need their advice, or do you just want to share your feelings? Your parents will be able to respond to you better if they are aware of your needs. If you absolutely don't want their advice, make sure you tell them that you're just wanting to share your feelings.

- **Prepare for the Worst-Case Scenario:** It is possible that your parents disagree with you. Have the conversation anyway. If you ask yourself "What's the worst that can happen after this discussion?" and you come to terms with, or accept that it may not change anything, then you will feel glad that you tried anyway.

- **Seek Professional Support:** There are several resources available that can help you navigate any sort of communication obstacles you may have with your parents.

Make sure you talk to your parents about your and their day; make sure you talk to them about the difficult things. It is a great way to continue your bond with them.

Don't Wait for Your Parents to Take the Lead

In the intricate dance of parent-child relationships, it's easy to fall into a familiar routine. We often wait for our parents to take the lead, both in conversations and in the broader aspects of life—and we even fall into this trap in adulthood, as well.

However, as we grow into adulthood especially, there comes a crucial realization—we hold equal responsibility for nurturing these connections. Waiting for your parents to steer the ship can lead to missed opportunities for understanding, bonding, and, most importantly, reciprocal love. Initiating conversations with them is a fundamental step in this journey.

Ask them about their day, their interests, or their thoughts. Be real with them as you would a friend and have an open conversation. By showing an active interest in their lives, you create an atmosphere of engagement and openness. This not only fosters stronger communication but also deepens the emotional connection between you.

Not waiting for your parents to take the lead means recognizing that love and communication are reciprocal, and that communication works two ways. When you actively participate in the exchange, it's a powerful demonstration of your love and appreciation for them. By initiating conversations, asking thoughtful questions, and expressing your own thoughts and experiences, you're building bonds that can span a lifetime. This proactive approach redefines your relationship with your parents. Instead of them as your authority figures, they can instead transition into a friendship relationship. This way, you all have mutual respect and love, where all parties contribute actively and evenly.

Offer Surprise Gestures

MY personality types tend to gravitate toward surprise gestures more than their CD counterpart, but everyone enjoys feeling special. No matter where your parents fall in the personality spectrum, it is almost certain that they can appreciate a random surprise gesture!

Cook For Them

There is an old saying, "A family that eats together, stays together". Cook for your family—either lunch or dinner—and enjoy it with them. This is a great opportunity to bond and spend quality time with each other.

Call Them Once a Week

If you are living far away from your parents, or at least far enough that weekly visits are out of the question, make sure you call them at least once a week. Take advantage of the good that technology can bring and make your parents feel as though you are still close to them while you're actually far away. Over the call, you can even opt to FaceTime or video call, and show them what's new with you rather than just telling them! This can be a great way to build closeness over a long distance.

Go with Them on a Trip

A change of weather and location is a natural way to refresh and rejuvenate. It would also give you a chance to unwind from the monotony of life. Take a small road trip with your parents or invite them on a weekend getaway.

Surprise Them with Gifts

No need to wait on special occasions. Sometimes the best gifts are "just because" gifts. They are your parents, and you can pamper them any moment you feel like. So, schedule a gift delivery to their home, or take it to them yourself, and make them smile from ear to ear.

Make a Surprise Visit to Them

If your parents always seem to want to spend time with you and you just haven't had a lot of time, consider making a surprise visit to them and spending the weekend. They would love it, and you could get a lot of much-needed bonding time. Spend the whole weekend with them (and if you have your own family now, take them with you), talk to

Pamper Them with a Spa Day

Just because they may not be used to it, or maybe have never even had it, don't sleep on the fact that a spa day is great for rejuvenating the soul! Sometimes our parents forget to take care of themselves. So, book a spa appointment for them so you can help them to relax and recharge their batteries. Consider booking a couples spa for them if they're still together so that they can spend some cozy time with one another.

Help Them with Housework

If you live with them, or nearby, the best way to pamper and surprise them is to help them with their daily or seasonal chores.

Say "I Love You" to Them

Mys especially love affirmation, but regardless, everyone wants to hear that they're loved. How many times have you expressed to your parents that you love them unconditionally? You can show them that you do by way of sweet gestures, but the biggest and best way—is to simply say "I love you."

Organize Family Get-Togethers

With some creativity and planning you can throw a stress-free family get-together. This can be anything from a family reunion, to just a regular ol' block party or holiday event. Taking this over for your parents can really alleviate some stress from them and also give you a chance to toss your creative flair into the mix and create new, refreshing family memories.

Planning is the key to organizing a successful family get-together. Work with your parents to determine who you want to invite. It may seem obvious, but if you have a large family, the guest list could become overwhelming, especially if you aren't used to hosting. Also make sure you get their input and expertise on a few traditions including what you should refresh, and what you should keep the same.

No matter how simple or grand the party is, hosting a family get-together is hard work but it can give you and your parents an amazing bonding experience as well.

Walk Down Memory Lane

Revisiting cherished memories and reliving special moments can be a powerful way to enhance emotional closeness with your parents. Remember, they have known you longer than anyone else has. It is important to highlight and remember major milestones in your life with them. Some great ways to walk down memory lane include:

- Organize your thoughts; it's important to know what you want to convey to them.

- Remember you can't take back what you write!

- Remember that this is an opportunity to share your story or feelings without distraction or interruption. Be authentic and genuine!

Make New Memories

While revisiting memories or places that are important to your family and your past is often an emotional experience, it is still important to make sure you're making new memories together! As you grow and mature, it's important to keep your relationship going with your parents.

Creating new memories with your parents is a wonderful way to strengthen your relationship. These moments can be cherished for a lifetime and can help you connect on a deeper level.

Travel Together

Exploring new destinations can be a fantastic way to bond with your parents. Whether it's a weekend getaway to a nearby town or an international adventure, traveling together allows you to share unique experiences and create lasting memories. Discovering new cultures, trying different cuisines, and exploring historic sites might be exactly what you all need to feel connected with each other and to get a jumpstart on new memories you can cherish forever.

Outdoor Adventures

Spend time in nature by going on hikes, camping trips, or nature walks. The great outdoors offers plenty of opportunities for bonding, and it's a chance to unplug from technology and enjoy each other's company. Consider kayaking or other on-the-lake adventures to kick it up a notch. If someone hasn't tried it, this experience can be even more enriching and mean even more!

Cooking and Baking

Preparing meals together can be a fun and delicious way to create memories. Consider trying to cook up a new recipe or bake homemade goodies, or even consider making it a game. A cook-off with judges is a great way to get the entire family involved. It's a win-win. You get quality time and yummy food! And if you're competitive, it may be a chance to really show off!

Attend Cultural Events

Explore your city—or a nearby city—and discover what sort of cultural scenes they have. Many cities have showcases of other cultures at various times throughout the year. Learn about some of these by searching online. You may find concerts, theater performances, art exhibits, or even full-blown cultural festivals that may be a ton of fun. Not only will these events provide their own opportunities to appreciate art and culture, but they can also be a great way to make memories with your family.

Document the Moments

Sometimes we don't remember everything as it was. Consider taking lots of photos and videos to enhance your memories and give you a tangible piece of the memory so that you can cherish that as well.

Volunteer Together

Giving back to the community by volunteering together is not only a meaningful way to bond but also a chance to make a positive impact on your community. Sharing this experience with your parents can be rewarding and create lasting memories centered around compassion and selflessness.

Delve into Mutual Hobbies

Journeying through life is all about exploration. While you may or may not have had a lot in common when you were growing up, there's still a whole world of possibilities to explore now that you're an adult.

Discovering and trying new things together is a chance to bond over shared interests and passions, whether you know you have them or not. The key to keeping a strong connection with your parents is to continually grow with them. What better way to bring forth some freshness than to find a fun new hobby you can partake in with them?

When exploring new activities to try, consider their interests and preferences. You can take turns choosing activities with them (whether it be the two of them together, or just you with one of them at a time), ensuring that you all have a say. Be open to trying things you may not have considered before; you might come to find that you enjoy something you never thought you could.

Whether it's trying a new cuisine, taking up a dance class, embarking on a road trip, or learning a new skill, the key is to approach these experiences with an open heart and mind and be willing to embrace the unknown. Know that at the end of the day, even if you don't enjoy the activity, you're doing something different with your parents that is sure to create memories and strengthen your relationship by just spending quality time together.

Keep in mind that CDs and Mys may enjoy different activities, but it's important for you all to try things even if you don't think you would enjoy them. You might surprise yourselves! To make this part of your regular scheduled dates, consider being the first to suggest it. Start with something you know they will enjoy to get the ball rolling.

If you want to experience a new activity with your CD parent, you could try:

- Starting a book club with them.
- Stretching it out with some yoga, whether at a studio or at home.
- Playing games or doing a puzzle together.
- Gardening together.
- Starting a collection.
- Beer brewing at home.
- Learning how to knit together.

Activities you may want to try with your MY parent include:

- Trying your hand at tie-dying.
- Learning a new language together.
- Cooking together.
- Going to an unknown band's concert.
- Trying a martial arts class.
- Go camping or biking.
- Rock climbing.
- Volunteering at a local soup kitchen.

Bring Them Thoughtful Gifts

If your parents were particularly generous with their gift-giving when you were a child, it may be time to pay some of that back. Bringing your parents gifts—especially ones you put a lot of thought into, may really be a great way to show your love for them. In fact, some personality types crave gifts.

But sometimes, we find that parents are not always easy to buy for. It can be difficult to find something they don't already have or that has real meaning.

So, what do you buy for your parents when they already have everything they want and can afford to buy whatever they don't have? That is where the word "thoughtful" comes into play! It is necessary to put some critical thinking into this situation. Some ideas include:

- A Personalized Pillow: Think about getting a pillow for your parents to put on their bed. It can have a quote or a photo of them together!

- A Personalized Mug: Do either or both of your parents drink coffee? Coffee mugs are some of the best gifts because everyone uses them. Customizing them with a photograph, a quote, or a hand-written note can go a long way—especially if they live further away than you'd like!

- **Kitchen Supplies:** Consider an apron or a cutting board. Customize these with your family name or the name of all of your parents' children. This could be a fun, clever, and intimate gift that they could keep (and use) for the rest of their lives.

- **A Doormat:** Personalized doormats are great because it's the first thing someone sees when they visit a home. Consider putting your family name as well as the family member names on this—that way your entire family is represented in the home.

- **A Cookie Jar:** Everyone needs a cookie jar for when kids and grandkids come over. Think of some of your parents' favorite things and personalize them!

- **A Wooden Clock or a Family Calendar:** Consider a customized clock with family members on it, or a calendar or family tree with everyone listed as well as their birthdays. These kinds of gifts are three-fold; they're informational (sometimes parents may need a little help remembering birthdays especially if you have a big family), they hold a practical use, and it's sweet and personalized so there's a sentimental aspect to it, too.

- **Art:** This can be something you found, something you made, or something you had made. Bring them some art to display and they'll think of you each and every time they pass it. Very few things can broadcast love like a piece of meaningful artwork...

The options are endless. Think of their favorite items; maybe it is a coffee mug; but maybe it's a baseball; maybe it's jewelry. Whatever sticks out, consider getting them that gift—and always consider making it personalized. A nice engraving or a photograph on an item goes a long way in turning a nice gift into an extraordinary one!

Offer to Help Them

Let's face it, our parents aren't getting any younger (and neither are we)! It's important to show your parents that you're appreciative of them and that you care enough to want to help them.

Around the House

Does it seem that even though you are out of the house, your parents are still super busy?

It's possible that your parents are still working hard running the home you grew up in and even maintaining their jobs; whether it be with just the two of them, or more if you have younger siblings still in the house.

You can show them how much you appreciate them by helping out with chores around the house when you have extra time on your hands (or even better, prioritize the time to help your parents). Ask them what you can do to help them if you're not sure where you might be most needed. They will likely appreciate your thoughtfulness!

If your family has a dog, a cat, a bird, a fish, or any animal, offer to help take care of them when you're hanging out around the house or visiting. You could also be a huge help and take them out for a walk, play fetch, or play with them with other toys.

More chores around the house you can do include taking out the trash, dusting unused areas they may not have gotten to in a while, or doing a bit of their laundry. As you know in your house, washing, drying, and folding clothes is time-consuming. Ask if you can help alleviate some of their chores once and a while to give them a break, even though it is possible you're overwhelmed with your own tasks at home.

Other ways you could help out inside the house could include cleaning the floors, helping with dinners (or bringing them dinner some nights), washing dishes, and even doing tasks that they may not know how to do or have the physical ability anymore. This could be electrical work, spring cleaning, or even organizing the garage.

Yardwork is one of those chores parents really need help with the older they get. Not only is it physically taxing, but the heat in the summer can be very dangerous to an older person. Grab a watering can and give your parents' thirsty plants a drink. If they have any indoor plants, carefully pour some water into the dirt around the base of the plant. If they have outdoor plants or a garden, you can use a hose to spray water directly into the dirt near the plants' roots. Remember that plants only need to be watered during certain times—if you don't know how to properly care for their plants, ask them! You never want to turn good-natured help into an inconvenience.

Singular Favors

Run errands for your parents from time to time, and if you're out and about and going to be near their neighborhood, call and ask them if they need anything.

And if you have younger siblings, offer to watch them from time to time so your parents can go out and do whatever they'd like.

Help Them Financially

If your parents are struggling financially, you can provide monetary support. But if you don't have the funds yourself, you can also offer non-monetary support to help improve their situation. Before you write them a check or even offer your advice, though, evaluate their needs and your capacity to meet them so that you know what you can offer.

Before your parents retire or face serious financial hardship, have an honest discussion with them about the challenges they're having or expect to have and the type of and extent of help they need or think they're going to need in the future. You can help your parents with their finances in various ways, whether that be through monetary support or through non-monetary support such as financial advice. The right approach will depend on where everyone is financially—you and them—and where everyone wants to be. Connecting them to a trusted financial advisor can also help facilitate these sorts of conversations.

Potential Challenges and How to Help

Everyone has their own set of challenges that can arise. A way to help your parents find theirs is to sit down with them and evaluate their habits.

If your parents have diligently saved, budgeted well, and are on track to cover their day-to-day expenses but expect to travel in retirement, their challenge might be having difficulty saving the extra needed for their travels. In this situation, non-monetary help might be sufficient for their needs. Working out a budget plan and how much they can actually afford in retirement is necessary.

On the flip side, if your parents are struggling financially in the short term, whether it's because they have unpaid debts, have lost their job, or had to take an early retirement, they may not be able to make ends meet now let alone have a comfortable retirement in the future.

They might prefer monetary support in this scenario, in which case it's useful to inquire about the amount they would need and what their plan would be long-term. Helping them in this situation both financially, and with advice, is crucial. If you don't have the funds to help them, consider other options.

Help Your Parents Financially Without Money

Not having the money to help your parents can be heartbreaking. But there are several ways to support them without opening your wallet:

- **Help Them Downsize:** If your parents are finding their current home unaffordable and there is wiggle room in the size of their home, it may make sense for them to downsize. Help them run the numbers on how much it might save to move to a smaller home and determine if it's worth it. Make sure that you factor in not only their mortgage and expenses but the cost of the move as well.

- **Guide Them Through Relocation:** It is possible that your parents are living in a location with high property taxes. It's also entirely possible that they moved there when you were a kid for the schools, and there is no reason for them to stay in that particular area anymore. Help your parents determine if there's an area better suited for them with a lower cost of living.

- **Ask Them to Move In:** If your parents can't afford to live independently, assess their health, your current lifestyle, and the other members of your household to determine whether they can live with you. Taking in your parents can have a profound positive impact on their finances, often freeing them from a mortgage, rental payments, and associated bills. However, make sure your partner or children are comfortable with this as it can create chaos if not done properly.

- **Create a Budget for Them:** It is entirely possible that your parents are seeking ways to stretch their money. This could be to have more money in savings or because they're struggling. Either way, one of the best ways to help them financially is to sit down with them and draft a basic budget that factors in their income and expenses every month.

- **Help with Maintenance or Repairs:** If your parents need help paying for car or home repairs, and you have the skills to do them, offer to do these repairs for them occasionally.

Key Takeaways

Open and honest communication is essential for maintaining a strong emotional bond with your parents. A strong emotional bond with your parents is the key to a successful relationship in adulthood. So, talk to your parents!

Regular conversations not only reduce stress but also contribute to identity formation, exploration, moral reasoning, and psychological maturity. Understand that it's common for parents and their adult children to have differing perspectives. This divergence can lead to a disconnect and make communication challenging. But participating in active listening and making an effort to understand their points of view can truly help, even when you disagree. Some great ways to nurture this emotional closeness with your parents are to:

- **Stop Waiting for Your Parents to Initiate Every Interaction:** Make sure that you're taking an active role in nurturing your relationship by asking them about their interests, thoughts, and experiences. This approach fosters engagement, openness, and mutual respect.

- **Surprise Them with Thoughtful Gestures:** Surprise your parents with thoughtful gestures, such as cooking for them, calling them regularly, planning trips, giving gifts, pampering them with a spa day, and helping with household chores. These gestures can reinforce your love and appreciation.

- **Plan Family** Get-Togethers: Organizing family gatherings, whether big or small, provides an opportunity to create lasting memories and strengthen family bonds. Collaborate with your parents on the planning process to maintain traditions while introducing new elements that keep it fresh and fun.

- **Walk Down Memory Lane:** Revisit cherished memories by looking at photo albums, creating a memory jar, revisiting special places, or watching home movies. These activities not only connect you through shared memories but also reinforce your emotional bond.

- **Express Your Love for Them:** Regardless of personality types, regularly express your love and affection for your parents by saying "I love you". This simple act can go a long way.

- **Create New Memories:** In addition to revisiting the past, actively engage in activities that foster new memories. Explore mutual hobbies, discover new interests, and bond over shared experiences.

- **Financial Assistance:** In cases where your parents need financial support, consider both monetary and non-monetary assistance. Create a budget, set limits, and plan for the long term while factoring in your own financial constraints as well.

Chapter Four

Celebrate Good Times

Life is made up of moments—some good, some bad, but all significant in shaping who we are as people. As adults, our relationships with our parents continue to evolve, and we often find ourselves craving deeper connections with them. One powerful way to nurture this sort of deep connection is by merely celebrating good times together. In this chapter, we'll explore the idea of bonding with parents through sharing moments of togetherness, such as inviting them over for dinner, letting them contribute where they can, and more.

This chapter will guide you on not only celebrating with your parents but also how to navigate the shifting dynamic and celebrate differently. You used to celebrate holidays with your parents because they threw parties, or because your teacher had you make them a Mother's Day or Father's Day gift. But now that you're an adult, you have a choice of how to celebrate. Using this guide, you can create a balance in a way that makes everyone happy and helps your parents feel like priorities.

Invite Your Parents Over for Dinner

Eating can be a wonderful bonding experience. Invite your parents over for dinner at your place—whether it's just with you or your family. This is a great opportunity to let them into your world as an adult.

Let Them Bring Something

If your parents ask what to bring, don't tell them "nothing". Have them bring something! Ask them to bring an appetizer or even a family-favorite dessert if they are up to it. Contributing to the meal might really make them feel special. However, if they're a bit older and have difficulty in the kitchen, maybe ask if they could bring a bottle of wine or another favorite beverage.

Get Them a Ride

Sometimes as your parents age, it's difficult to get them to visit. This could be due to a multitude of factors, but for many, the older our parents get, the less likely they are comfortable driving far, or at night. Advanced services such as Uber or Lyft (or even a run-of-the-mill taxi company), can make the task a lot more simple. You and/or your partner no longer have to worry about them getting to you—which can mean more time to prepare your meal!

Let Your Guests Help

Delegating or assigning tasks to your parents or others who may be attending, such as peeling vegetables, grating cheese, or tossing a salad, is sometimes necessary, especially if you want to entertain as well! Your parents may make this a special opportunity to teach their all-important kitchen skills and pass something down to you (or even your children), too.

Prepare Alternative Activities

If either of your parents (or other guests) aren't into being in the kitchen while the meal is prepared, you may want to prepare additional activities, such as having some sport on, or bringing out a deck of cards! Choose something fun so that it doesn't feel like a chore.

Choose a Meal That is Tasty but Recognizable

Older generations have their favorite dishes, so beware of deviating too much from that. If you're looking for a dish that is healthy—you can modify a family favorite to include healthy ingredients. For example, consider ground turkey instead of ground beef, or Greek yogurt instead of cream. These small swaps won't jeopardize the taste of pickier parents who may be used to the original dishes and can also be what you and your family need for your appetites.

Share Stories and Laugh Together

Sharing stories helps us find common ground with people, and our parents are no exception. Turn everyone's individual story into a storybook; add family trees, photographs, memories, and quotes from family members as well as any funny life moments or favorite things you think are worth mentioning. You can make it specific and focus on an individual—maybe write your dad as the hero of the story or write a section of your parents' first meeting. Anything! This is your family's story; do what you want! Other creative ways to share your stories include:

- Recipes—create a family cookbook!

- Have a family journal.

- Make family movies/videos and send them to one another as things happen worthy of sharing.

Host Mutual Social Events or Gatherings

In the same manner as inviting your family to dinner, make it a point to have mutual social events or gatherings. Grill out with them at a cookout. Have them invite their friends, and you invite yours! This is a great way to get the generations together and learn from one another.

Celebrate Important Holidays or Anniversaries Together

Not only is it important to celebrate important holidays and anniversaries because it helps you feel closer to one another, but it is also necessary to show your appreciation and admiration to your family, where they came from; and where they're going from here. For example, your parents made you—celebrating their anniversary is in essence celebrating the beginning of your family.

When it Makes Sense, Combine Events

Combine your childhood family's holidays with your new family's. If you're married, see if your spouse's family can join, and suggest hosting, since that would give both families neutral ground. If this isn't possible, though, then maybe suggest sharing the holidays. You and your partner (and your children if you have them) could go to one of your family's gatherings in the morning and switch it up in the evening (if distance allows). If distance is an obstacle, consider alternating holidays!

Do what works best for your family, but either way, try to incorporate your family with your partner (and children if you have them) with the family you grew up with. It makes holidays a lot more special and festive. Make these sorts of things a tradition and do it every year! A word of advice: If you're taking on the position of hosting an event for a family member (or your spouse's family member), it is important to ask questions. Most families have ingrained structures and dynamics. You don't want to step on anyone's toes, so make sure you're respecting traditions and ask permission before you take the lead. You know your own family best, and there is no one better to determine what is best for everyone when it comes to your next big event.

Create Memory Gifts

Memory gifts are a great, personalized option that is sure to make your parents feel good. They're a great way to memorialize good times. Types of memory gifts include personalized photo albums, lockets with photographs inside, and picture ornaments. These gifts are great for when you want to feel connected to a loved one, have a piece to remember your loved ones by, preserve your memories, and keep a memoir to pass on to future generations.

Celebrate Them "Just Because"

When it comes to gestures and surprises for your parents, it is important to note that in celebrating them—and good times—it should be considered to make an effort to celebrate them "just because".

You don't need a holiday or a special occasion to send your mother flowers or ask your dad to go fishing. You can do it at any time, and for no reason in particular—just "because". Consider your parents and their individual needs or desires, and try to cater to them. Take them out, keep them in, it doesn't matter. What matters is doing something special for each of them individually in a way that they will appreciate uniquely.

Thank Them for Doing Their Best

If you grew up feeling like you didn't have a great childhood, like many, do your best not to put all the blame on your parents. It is likely that any poor parenting was due to a poor education and/or an unclear understanding of how the world works, as well as the psyche. This is usually also due to poor parenting from their parents before them.

Of course, it is important to communicate your feelings with your parents, but it is equally important that we don't blame them for whatever situation we may find ourselves in. In adulthood, the sheer fact is that we all have a choice; and we always will have one. Parents are supposed to teach you which choices are the wisest to make, and which ones you should avoid making. That is the philosophy that being a parent is all about. However, when our parents are ill-equipped to make those choices themselves, that at times leaves us with little resources. So even if you struggled with your childhood, remember to thank your parents for doing their best and giving you:

- A big family breakfast.

- Cookouts and outdoor games.

- Dinner and dessert.

Of course, you can get your parents gifts, too, but remember, the most important aspect of the day is spending it together. If distance is a factor and it isn't possible to visit, send them gifts and hand-written letters/cards or even a personalized video/video call.

Recognize Their Achievements and Yours—Together

Life is a journey filled with accomplishments and milestones. Celebrate your parents' achievements along with your own. This can be by celebrating them in helping you achieve your goals, such as being a support to you when you graduate college, or it can be their own individual accomplishments. Celebrate that promotion your mom or dad just got; celebrate their retirement; celebrate that big purchase they just made. Whatever their achievements, recognize them, and celebrate them.

Share your successes and goals with them, too. Let them know when you're doing well so they aren't only there for you in the tough times, but also the good! Let them flood you with love. Doing these things together is a powerful way to celebrate life in general—but is also good for celebrating your parents and the good times you have together and individually.

Tell Your Parents You Love Them

In the hustle and bustle of daily life, it's easy to take your parents for granted. Take a moment to pause and tell your parents that you love them. Whether it's through a heartfelt conversation in person, a simple "I love you" note or text, or an unexpected hug or gesture, expressing your love openly and regularly is a powerful way to celebrate your relationship. It reinforces the fact that your affection is constant, regardless of the circumstances. Keep them a priority and your bond will always be there.

Share Life-Altering Moments with Them (Even the Bad Ones)

It's easy to share the good news. That new promotion, that big car or home purchase, the engagement—these are all exciting and worth celebrating. But make sure you're being real with your parents. Tell them when that breakup happens, when you lose your job, or when you're having trouble making bills and you think something financially detrimental may happen.

Sharing your life moments with your family brings you closer together. Not only can they offer their advice to you, but they can also be a shoulder to lean on in times of distress.

Key Takeaways

Celebrating good times with your parents is a meaningful way to deepen your adult relationship with them. Inviting your parents over for dinner is an opportunity to share your world and experiences, fostering a stronger bond. Allow them to contribute to the meal, share stories, and involve them in the process, passing down family traditions and cherished skills. Celebrating your parents is an ongoing process and isn't limited to special occasions. By expressing your love and gratitude with them all the time you can strengthen your emotional connection and enhance your familial bond in general. Great ways to continue to celebrate them and the good times are to:

- **Invite Your Parents for Dinner:** Hosting your parents for a meal at your place is a great way to strengthen your adult relationship and let them into your world. Don't forget to choose familiar, yet tasty meals that cater to their preferences.

- **Let Them Contribute:** When your parents ask what to bring, allow them to contribute to the meal by bringing an appetizer, dessert, or a beverage. It makes them feel special and involved.

- **Assist with Transportation When You Can:** For aging parents, if you can't pick them up yourself, offer transportation options such as Uber or Lyft to make it easier for them to visit.

- **Prepare Activities:** Plan activities for those who may not be involved in the cooking process. Having the TV on or a deck of cards out will make the gathering a bit more enjoyable for everyone.

- **Share Stories and Laugh Together:** Sharing family stories is an excellent way to find common ground with your parents. Extend this to other family members as well to create a fun game!

- **Create Memory Gifts:** Celebrating good times means remembering them. Consider putting your family stories into books, movies, games, or even memorializing photographs on items to preserve and pass down your family's wisdom and experiences.

- **Host Mutual Social Events and Spend Holidays Together:** Beyond dinners, organize social gatherings and celebrations, such as holiday parties, to bring generations together and facilitate learning from one another. It doesn't have to just be family, either. Make it a real party by inviting your parents' friends and your friends. It gives everyone a chance to mingle and enjoy one another. Also, remember to spend holidays and certain anniversaries with your parents, as it is not only a way to show appreciation but also to create meaningful family traditions. And do not forget them on Mother's and Father's Days, even if you're a parent yourself!

- **Tell Your Parents You Love Them:** Regularly tell them you love them. Even though it may seem obvious, the words "I love you" hold lots of power in your connection to one another.

- **Share Life-Altering Moments:** Don't exclude your parents from important events in your life, both good and bad. Let them be part of your journey so that they can continue to offer their support and guidance.

Celebrating good times with your parents is an ongoing, meaningful practice that can lead to a deeper, more fulfilling adult relationship and create lasting memories for your family.

Chapter Five

Appreciate Them for Who They Are

In this chapter, we delve into the essential elements of fostering a deeper and more meaningful connection with your parents by merely appreciating them for who they are. As adults, we often focus on building independent lives and even possibly blame our parents for certain things we feel we lack. However, appreciating them for who they are is fundamental in growing closer to them. And in order to truly appreciate them for who they are, you must come to the realization that your parents are human. In this section, we delve into the reality that despite our childish thoughts when we were kids, our parents aren't superheroes. They're only human.

Get to know them for who they are, asking them questions to truly understand them. This chapter will help you to be open and receptive and to truly get to know your parents. It will also teach you how you might forgive and move forward from issues you might have from your childhood.

Celebrate Their Emotional Strengths

Celebrating the emotional strengths each person brings to the familial table is essential for bonding and growth. To love your parents more effectively, resonate with them emotionally.

Identify Emotional Strengths and Compliment Them

Take the time to identify and acknowledge the unique emotional strengths each of you has. CDs often bring introspection, empathy, and stability, while MYs may contribute enthusiasm, spontaneity, and optimism. Recognize how your emotional strengths complement your parents and vice versa.

CDs can provide a stabilizing presence during challenging times, while MYs can infuse energy and positivity into the mix where negativity could normally take over. are part of people's identity and your parents have them just like everyone else. Learn to appreciate these differences because oftentimes these personality differences correspond with emotional differences too.

Your parents having different emotional strengths than you is actually quite a good thing because oftentimes the relationship becomes more stable over time as a result. This is because each of you can feed off the other's energy. Where one person lacks, the others can cover the bill, and vice versa.

Express Gratitude

Regularly express your gratitude for your parents and their emotional strengths. If you've had a particularly bad day and your MY parent(s) has supported you and breathed a fresh, upbeat, and optimistic breath of fresh air into your lungs, make sure you acknowledge that and express your gratitude to them. Perhaps you feel like your life has found its way rolling down a tumultuous road, and they bring stability where you don't feel it anywhere else. Let them know how their qualities have positively impacted you. A simple "thank you" can go a long way.

Quality Time

Spend quality time together to explore and appreciate each of your emotional strengths. Engage in activities that allow you to showcase your respective qualities. For example, CDs can guide deep, meaningful conversations, while MYs can plan exciting, adventurous outings. During this quality time, it may also be important to open communication about emotions and feelings. Encourage each other to express how you're feeling and why. CDs may prefer in-depth discussions, while MYs might use more expressive and spontaneous forms of communication. Strive for a balance between emotional intensity and stability. Recognize that both intense emotional experiences and calm, grounding moments have their place in a healthy relationship.

Learn from Each Other to Obtain Emotional Growth

Embrace the opportunity to learn from each other's emotional strengths. CDs can learn to embrace spontaneity and adaptability from MYs, meanwhile, MYs can benefit from the introspection and depth of CDs. Commit to growing emotionally as a family by lending your emotional strengths to each other. Explore ways to develop and refine your emotional strengths, both individually and collectively.

Understand That They're Human—Just Like You

Sorry to break it to you, but your parents are only human, just like you. Of course, everyone has different experiences with their parents, and some may not have the best relationship with either one or both of their parents. It's possible to hold and carry a great deal of resentment toward them because of that. However, it is important as we grow to learn to forgive them.

It's important to forgive and let go of the hurt you carry from the past. It may not be the easiest thing to do, but it's necessary.

We forget the fact that our parents were normal people before they were our parents. Obviously, we've never experienced them outside of being our parents and therefore we don't tend to take this into consideration. However, it is important to not only know that but to understand what it means. We have to humanize our parents.

We cannot be overly critical of them and the mistakes they make—especially when they don't know any better. In fact, we have to extend the same level of grace that we hope is extended to ourselves.

If you've become a parent by now then it may be easier to relate, but if not, try to empathize. Your parents were young once, and they were inexperienced. They had no idea how to be parents. They may not have even wanted to become parents at the time of your conception. It isn't a shock that young adults often have unplanned pregnancies. By shifting your mindset to this, it may be easier to understand that it could be entirely possible that your parents were just young, inexperienced, and clueless, like many parents. And there is no one-size-fits-all parenting guide.

Frustration often lies in the fact that we criticize our parents for not teaching us something or not doing something we feel they should have. The fundamental truth is that it is entirely possible that their parents simply may not have known. In the world of information overload, at any given time we can find out anything we want to know right at our fingertips. However, it is possible that our parents didn't possess the same advantages as we do, and it's easy to forget that—and inadvertently hold our parents to an impossible standard.

When You Start to Realize that They're People

Now that we are all grown up, and we realize that our parents are people, too, we can have the opportunity to learn about them as individuals. They had their own life before we came into the picture. Now, we get to learn about all the different things they did when they were younger (possibly even your age). Be prepared to discuss boundaries before this and what you're ok with them sharing, because you just might find that there are some things you'd prefer not to know about your parents when they were younger!

Your Parents Are Not Perfect, and Neither Are You

In learning that your parents are real people, just like you, you learn that they aren't perfect. They are far from it, in fact, no matter how much you wanted to believe they were when you were a child. Indeed, they are not the superheroes we may have thought they were, but they're still pretty wonderful. They have each likely made their fair share of mistakes in the past. But that's okay—because haven't we all? We are all just figuring this out as we go along, and we all just keep making big ol' life mistakes together. It's all part of the journey, and it's all part of growing.

You Don't Have All the Answers, and Your Parents Didn't Either

One thing that we know for certain about ourselves is that we are new to this whole adulthood thing, and adulting is pretty dang hard sometimes. Looking at yourself in the mirror, it's pretty simple to say, "I do not have a clue what's going on". None of us have all the answers, even if we like to think we do. And now that you understand your parents are people too, it's safe to say that they don't have a clue what's going on either. They do not have all the answers, no matter how much we would all like to think they do or did. Of course, when you were a child, the fact of it was that your parents likely fixed everything and somehow made everything right. But the sad truth is—they were just figuring things out as they went along. Just like you are now.

They're Still Growing and Learning, Just Like You Are

It's easy to get it into your head that, since your parents are older and wiser, they're definitely finished growing as individuals and are set in their ways. And of course, that may be true in some ways, but your parents have just as much capability of growing and learning as you do. They are still experiencing life and learning from it, each and every day. As people, we should always strive to learn how to be better versions of ourselves and improve. Your parents are doing this, too, so help them grow and learn as you continue to appreciate them for who they are and what they bring to the table.

You May Be More Alike Than You Thought

It's likely that as you grew up and hit your adolescent years, you swore to yourself that you would never end up like your parents. Spoiler alert, you're probably more alike than you thought. Of course, there are exceptions to this, but finding common ground can help you truly appreciate your parents for who they are. Have you ever found yourself saying a phrase that they used to say? That's usually the beginning, but the fact of it is that you are a piece of them, and it is entirely possible that all of you have more common ground than any of you ever knew or anticipated before.

Break the Cycle

Instead of chastising our parents about what they did and did not do correctly, we should recognize one thing: our parents are likely a product of their upbringing, just as their parents were before them. There is no guide on how to be the perfect parent and so this means our parents learned as they went along, just as every other parent does. What was learned in the moment then gets passed down. Some may have experienced domestic violence in their upbringing and in turn, saw it as normal behavior and may have never been taught self-regulation in regard to their emotions because of it. Then, when we got older, we carried out those same beliefs due to what was indirectly taught to us as children. This is also true of being exposed to poverty, abuse, and excessive drug and/or alcohol use. A lot of the toxic behaviors that we carry with us now have been passed down from generation to generation and it's up to us to break the cycle and stop passing it to our children. That starts with forgiveness.

However, possessing this guide already shows that you're choosing to shift your mindset, which is something that has to be done and is the first step to forgiveness if you feel your parents have made mistakes.

Generational curses are a real thing. Much of the dysfunction that exists is learned and passed down. Many of the toxic traits we possess are inherited. This is not an excuse, but simply an explanation. We have the authority to make the decision to change it—so understand your parents are human, forgive them, and break the cycle for the future.

Ask Them About Their Past

It's easy to see your parents as one-dimensional figures limited to their roles of "Mom" or "Dad," and it's easy to forget that they had an entire life before you were born. We get caught up in the day-to-day noise of life, the transactional updates and small talk, or the habitual avoidance of controversial topics, and this means that we sometimes forget to really get to know our loved ones on a deeper level. If you are looking to get to know your parents in a whole new light, strengthen or reset your relationship, and connect your children to their grandparents. Having some insight into their past is a great place to start!

Playing the "20 Questions" game might be a great way to get to know them—and them you! It is a great, easy, and fun game to play to open the door to discovering people for who they are. Play it at the next family gathering so that friends and family can all participate! You'll be amazed at the new light through which you will all see each other.

20 Questions to Ask Your Parents:

- What were your favorite toys as a child?

- What was your favorite lunch when you were in school?

- What's the first major news story you remember?

- Did you have a secret fort or a tree house?

- What was your favorite room in the house you grew up in?

- What's a song that you most associate with your teenage years?

- What did you want to be when you grew up?

- What was the best thing about your wedding day?

- What are the most important lessons you have learned from life?

- How are you different from your parents?

- How did you learn you were going to be a parent for the first time?

- What was your favorite activity as a young adult?

- What happened on the day I was born?

- What is the funniest story you have about being a parent?

- What's one of the prouder moments you can remember as a parent?

- What's one of the most memorable gifts you've ever received?

- What is something that you learned after it was too late?

- What's the hardest choice you've ever had to make and who helped you make it?

- What first exposure to a breakthrough in technology will you never forget?

- What is your favorite thing to do in your spare time now?

Ask Them About Their Future

Even if your parents are in good health physically, emotionally, and financially, the conversation about their future needs to happen. Circumstances can change in the blink of an eye, and it is in your best interest to find out what sorts of plans your parents have before an emergency even happens. If they have no idea what they want to do, encourage them to let you start helping them make some decisions.

This isn't just in regard to a future funeral, but also what happens if one gets sick, or injured—or even worse, both.

You might be saying to yourself, "I don't even want to think about that!"—and that's completely okay. But ask yourself, which of these is more difficult? - Talking about a vison of the future, or finding yourself making decisions for a parent who is unable to decide for themselves? Having a conversation about finances, or paying thousands of dollars out of your own pocket for medical care for a parent? Asking your parents about their current health and their future medical outlook, or being unprepared and having to juggle caring for your family with caring for one parent—or both?

Avoiding these conversations can lead to being unprepared and tasked with holding things together that feel as though they're falling apart. You and your parents may be emotional, tired, or unable to discuss this at first, so make sure you take it slowly. If you haven't had these conversations, you may not have a clear direction about what to do, what they want, or how to even start discovering the kinds of services they will need should something happen.

Making a plan doesn't mean you'll always need it, but it's always better to have it and not need it than need it and not have it. In these situations, we hope we never have to use it; however, with the population living longer, some type of care will be needed at some point, even if it is only needed for a short time.

By keeping the lines of communication open, the plan can be changed as circumstances change. This keeps everyone involved feeling more confident and comfortable because they are able to establish what their role is and have a shared vision of the desired outcomes.

Become Their Friend

As we discussed earlier, parent-child relationships can become friendships. However, like all relationships, they can't thrive without open and honest communication. It might take some time to figure out just how open and honest you want to be, and that's normal. And since no two families are the same, only you and your parents can decide which things you choose to have in the line of your communication. If your parents are toxic, then you might not want to be close to them, and that's also okay. Or, if they're more conservative about certain things, it's perfectly fine for you—and them—to request that some items in your lives be off-limits in your communication.

That said, if you want to be close to your parents, then you're going to have to sit down and talk to them. It will likely be uncomfortable at first, but as long as everyone is respectful, can change your relationship with them in the best ways. Here are a few things you should consider telling your parents about if you haven't already:

- **What Kind of Relationship You Want to Have with Them:** Even for close families, conversations like this can be challenging to respectfully navigate. If you want to have a close and healthy relationship with your parents, then you need to make the time to sit down with them and discuss what kind of relationship you want to have. Decide how open you want to be with your parents—and how open you want them to be with you—and then talk it out. Be respectful, express your boundaries and goals for your relationship with them as clearly as possible, and do your best not to be judgmental just as you expect them to not be judgmental with you. It is impossible for you all to agree on everything, but if you can learn how to respectfully communicate with each other anyway, you might be surprised by how little your conflicting ideals matter.

- **Your Sexuality:** Your sexuality is your business and your business alone. You do not ever have to open up about it if you don't want to. Don't pressure yourself. However, if you do want to be close to your parents, it is recommended that you be honest with them about it. That said, never put yourself in a situation that is dangerous or puts your four walls at risk.

- **Your Spirituality:** It is entirely possible that you and your family have the same spiritual views. If that's the case, that's great! You can skip over this item altogether. However, if you do end up holding different spiritual beliefs from your parents, then you should consider opening up to them about it.

- **Your Political Views:** This one can be one of the more tricky items to discuss. Unless you and your parents have the same political views, which is almost nearly impossible, it can be difficult to get them to understand your point of view. On a broad scale, many people have the same political views as their parents, but when individual policies come into play, you may find that you differ enough to cause debate. Debate isn't always a negative thing, but it can cause chaos if proper communication isn't used in your discussions.

- **Your Mental Health:** Opening up about mental health issues is really difficult if you struggle. Unless your parents contribute to your mental health struggles, it is recommended you open up to them about it. They should be aware of stressors, and triggers, and also be given the opportunity to love and support you through your ailments.

Key Takeaways

This chapter underscored the significance of appreciating your parents for who they are. It is a fundamental step toward forging deeper and more meaningful connections, as it encourages individuals to celebrate the emotional strengths that each family member brings to the table, no matter their personality type. By recognizing and acknowledging these unique emotional qualities, family members can resonate with one another and learn to lean on each other for support. Whether one person possesses introspection and empathy or enthusiasm and spontaneity, these differences in emotional strengths can complement each other and contribute to a more stable family dynamic. When one person falters, the others can be found with their own strengths to offer support and advice. Expressing gratitude for these emotional strengths is essential. A simple "thank you" can have a profound impact and help your parents see that they are, indeed, appreciated.

In addition, show them your appreciation by spending quality time with them. This time can not only show them that they matter, but it also will give you all a chance to learn about each other's emotional strengths and learn from them.

As you learn and grow together, it is important to let go of negative behaviors or traits passed down through generations. Break the cycle and offer forgiveness if your parents did wrong in the past. This chapter is all about appreciating your parents for who they are now, and who they are striving to be. By recognizing the patterns and behaviors that need to change and taking steps to break them, individuals can contribute to healthier family dynamics for the future.

And finally, the chapter focuses on having an open conversation with your parents about their past, their favorite memories, and their future plans as a way to connect on a deeper level and understand their desires and needs. Ultimately that openness is the key to truly building a strong parent-child relationship. Share yourself and your personal life and understand theirs. Share with them the deepest and most vulnerable areas if you can. Areas such as politics, sexuality, spirituality, and your mental health are all heavy topics that can offer a chance to grow even closer as a family.

Chapter Six

Boundaries and Opinions

In this chapter, we delve into the importance of setting boundaries. Whether you cohabitate with your parents or not, it's crucial to establish clear boundaries and engage in open discussions about expectations. This doesn't matter if you've moved in with them, or they have moved in with you. This guide will teach you how to properly set boundaries with them in your adulthood. Communication and respect for each other's boundaries are crucial for maintaining a peaceful coexistence. This guide will also discuss taking your parents' advice, as it is likely still quite valuable to you, and it will teach you that it is equally important to listen and respect their input after they have given it. Don't hesitate to ask for help when needed and communicate your feelings honestly. When misunderstandings occur, give your parents the benefit of the doubt, recognizing their limitations. Avoid using offensive language to maintain mutual respect. Lastly, this guide will teach you how to set boundaries that prioritize "you" time for self-care and personal growth and engage in activities that recharge and rejuvenate you.

Set Boundaries for Your Parents During Major Transitions

It's critical to speak to your parents about specific ground rules. If you are going to live with your parents, it's crucial to discuss the living arrangements, rules, and responsibilities beforehand to help prevent misunderstandings. We all want comfortable living situations, and open communication is key here. Consider questions such as:

- How much should I contribute?

- How long will we be in the same household?

- How much privacy is needed?

Clear communication not only helps you share your intentions but also prevents unwanted surprises and potentially strained relationships as a result. Establishing boundaries within the home, such as the need for personal space and when it is appropriate to interact with one another can help maintain a peaceful space. By communicating effectively and respecting each other's boundaries, you can build trust and strengthen your relationship with your parents.

In a regular roommate situation, it's normal to come to some sort of agreement on rules for the house as well as the people residing within. It's normal to discuss responsibilities and expectations—especially before moving in together. So, do the same with your parents, whether you're still living with them as an adult, you're looking to move back in, or they're moving in with you. Set aside time to have a serious conversation on any past issues that might need to be dealt with, obstacles you anticipate in the future, and how your day-to-day living situation will look.

For example, work out how much each party is expected to pay in rent, bills, and other costs. Work out that plan ahead of time and try to get a game plan on how long you intend on living together.

If you're not living with your parents at all, it's still crucial that you set some sort of boundary—especially as you transition into adulthood. Boundaries can be established at any point, from when you move out on your own, to living with a spouse or partner, to having children—any of these transitions would require some visitation to the boundary discussion.

Ask for Advice and Listen When They Give It

While you can set boundaries for your parents and vice versa, it's important to note during your boundary discussion the importance of respecting one another's advice. For example, if you're going to ask for advice, don't ignore them when they give it to you. That shows you don't respect them or their time. Going to your parents for advice may seem like second nature, or, on the flip side, it may sound absolutely horrifying to you. Either way, your parents will feel important and trusted if you go to them for advice every once in a while.

Know That There's Nothing Wrong with Asking for Help

As much as your pride can tell you that it's terrible asking for help, it's not. Everyone needs help every now and then just like everyone needs advice. Remember, those who are successful in life are not those who don't have obstacles, but they're the ones who are able to find the resources and tools to make those obstacles disappear.

When You Need Help, You be the One to Bring It Up

Pick a low-key moment. Don't make it out to be some big, dramatic thing. It's always easier to talk to someone when everyone feels comfortable and relaxed.

Explain How You're Feeling

Make sure if you're having an issue with something that you really let your parents know what you're actually feeling. Describe what it is that you're truly having trouble with and how it is affecting you. If you don't quite know how to communicate it, then tell them in calm and considerate language. For example, "I'm not sure what I'm feeling, but I don't feel like myself".

Maybe even let them know certain symptoms you have and in what way you don't feel like yourself. Maybe you're tired lately; maybe irritable. Or maybe you know exactly what's wrong. Whatever the case, communicate what you can so that they can better help you.

Say You Want Help

Don't get caught up trying to analyze or explain the whys especially when you don't know. Let them know you need help and to what extent you feel you need it. Everyone gets nervous or upset sometimes, but let them know if it is more serious than that. If it isn't, then get their advice as you normally would. But if it seems like something more serious, don't be afraid to talk to them about helping you get with a professional. At the end of the day, trust your parents. Let them know you need help, and let them help you decide what sort of help you need.

If You Need To, Try Again Later

Sometimes, we can't bring ourselves to tell our parents—or anyone—what is wrong. And sometimes, when we're ready to talk, who we want to talk to isn't available. Sometimes it's not a good time. If that's the case, don't fret. It's entirely possible that they just don't have the time at the moment; let yourself know that it's okay to try again later.

If you feel as though your parents are brushing you off, try talking to them at a different time. Sometimes people just need a little time to understand where you're coming from. If it's necessary, ask them when they may be free to talk.

Don't Wait if You Need Help

The sooner you ask for help, the sooner you'll start feeling better, so don't put the conversation off. You'll be proud of yourself afterward and likely feel less alone. And that in and of itself can feel like a major relief.

Ultimately, don't be ashamed to ask your parents for advice. Communicate with them as clearly as you can. Let them know you need help if you do and help set the expectation. Let them know what you want from them. Remember, if you ask for advice, be prepared to accept it and take it. You don't have to follow it to a T, but at least acknowledge the time and care that was taken in order to give it to you.

Give Them the Benefit of the Doubt During Misunderstandings

People are typically doing the best they can. Generally speaking, it's safe to assume that if a person could do better at any point, they would. As adults, we sometimes have difficulty regulating our emotions. It is often referred to as "adult temper tantrums" and it refers to when an adult becomes completely ungrounded. If those people had the necessary tools in place, don't you think they could do better, they would?

Giving people the benefit of the doubt is really all about trust, and we need to trust our parents. If you're a trusting person, you would likely expect others to be trusting as well. And of course, when you do trust someone and they break that trust, it is upsetting. You may think yourself naïve, but in truth, it's just that your expectations of others can never be based on your own personal journey. Just because you have certain tools or resources in place, doesn't mean others do. Your life and your actions are not their lives and their actions.

Just like your parents' actions are not your actions and vice versa. It is important that we understand that our parents did not have the same upbringing as we did. They also may not be equipped in the same way that we are. Always give them the benefit of the doubt knowing that if they could have done better in any given situation or misunderstanding, they likely would have.

Avoid Being Offensive with Your Language

Use bad language sparingly around your parents. Using foul language around your parents, even as an adult, could be considered or looked upon as disrespectful and can have several implications. First and foremost, it's essential to recognize that your parents have played a significant role in shaping your values and behaviors in your adulthood. Using offensive language can be perceived as a disregard for the values they instilled in you during your childhood. Maintaining a level of respect in your interactions with them can be seen as a sign of appreciation for the guidance they've provided throughout your entire upbringing.

You don't want to make them uncomfortable, either, and even though you aren't a little kid anymore, you will always be their child. Parents might feel uncomfortable, hurt, or disrespected when they hear their children use offensive or derogatory words. It can create a barrier in open and honest communication, making it challenging to discuss important matters or express genuine emotions due to the way that they feel about the entire situation. By refraining from foul language, you help create a more conducive environment for meaningful conversations and ensure that your relationship remains built on mutual respect. Remember, as adults, you can express yourself effectively without resorting to offensive language, no matter how colorful it is and how habitual it has become in other areas of your life.

Remember, there is a time and a place for everything, and generally speaking, offensive language, whether it's around your parents or in any social context, can have several negative consequences. You wouldn't curse like a sailor in the middle of a business presentation. Maintaining a respectful and considerate manner of speech is important in certain contexts, and this includes conversations with your parents.

Don't Forget "You" Time

In setting appropriate boundaries with your parents, it's important to schedule "you" time and make sure that they respect that you need it. Taking "you" time is a crucial aspect of maintaining a healthy and balanced life. You can't give your all to others and give yourself nothing. While nurturing relationships with your parents (and everyone else) is essential, it's equally important to prioritize self-care and personal time. Here are some reasons why "you" time is vital:

Recharge and Rejuvenate

Caring for others, especially aging parents, and tending to family responsibilities can be emotionally and physically taxing. To be the best version of yourself and provide effective support to your loved ones, you need moments of solitude to relax, de-stress, and regain your energy. Whether it's engaging in a hobby or even just meditating, "you" time can give you a chance to completely refresh and feel rejuvenated.

Your Own Identity

Personal time ensures that you maintain your identity and interests. It is easy to get caught up in your responsibilities, and if you're caring for an elderly parent, it's almost even more critical that you have more self-reflective time at your disposal due to how emotionally taxing it can be. Dedicating time to activities you've always enjoyed really solidifies you being your own person. It can help bring satisfaction and fulfillment. Whereas, not giving in to your own personal desires can easily dwindle your identity down and even mold it into the people you surround yourself with instead. This isn't healthy and can create a co-dependent attitude and persona.

Overall Health and Wellbeing

Some of your "you" time can be focused on physical fitness, too. It doesn't always have to be a mental health break. Engaging in physical fitness activities will improve your physical and mental health. Engaging in self-care activities of all shapes and sizes matters to your overall health. Reading, spa days, playing sports—it all allows you to focus on physical fitness, mental health, and personal growth. These can enhance your self-esteem and provide you with a sense of achievement, ultimately making you a more confident and content caregiver for your parents. It's all about give and take and don't forget that you need to take a little time for yourself in order to give yourself.

Here are some activities you can consider when you feel you need some time to yourself to recharge:

- Read a Book: Reading is a great way to escape into different worlds, gain knowledge, and unwind. Choose a book that interests you and get lost in it!

- Exercise: Physical activity is an excellent stress reliever and mood booster. Whether it's going for a jog, practicing yoga, pumping iron, or taking a dance class, find an exercise routine that you enjoy and be consistent with.

- Meditation: Spend time meditating or practicing mindfulness to relax your mind, reduce stress, and improve your mental well-being.

- Hobbies: Reconnect with or even consider discovering new hobbies that bring you joy. It could be painting, gardening, cooking, playing a musical instrument, canoeing, or gaming! Anything that you enjoy that would help you decompress is valuable.

- Take a Nature Walk: Spending time in nature can be incredibly rejuvenating. Take a walk in a park, hike through the woods, or simply enjoy the outdoors to clear your mind.

- Spa Day: Treat yourself to a spa day, a massage, a manicure/pedicure, or even just a DIY spa experience at home with a warm bath, facial masks, and relaxation.

- Travel: Plan a short getaway or a vacation to explore new places, cultures, and cuisines.

- Listen to Music: Music has a profound impact on your mood and can be a major therapeutic venture. Create playlists of your favorite songs or attend live music events to really get your fill!

- Journaling: Writing in a journal can help you reflect, set goals, and express your thoughts and emotions. It's a therapeutic way to process your feelings. You can also get creative and write your own story; something that can unleash your creativity and give you an outlet.

- Watch Movies or TV Shows: Sometimes, there's nothing like vegging out on the couch and watching your favorite movie or TV series. You work hard; enjoy the downtime!

Key Takeaways

In this chapter, we learned the significance of establishing boundaries with your parents. We also learned that it isn't blanketly suggested for only those sharing a living space with them. No matter what, setting boundaries with your parents is a must. Being clear with them and engaging in open discussions about expectations is crucial, as it helps prevent misunderstandings and promotes a peaceful environment within your relationship.

When living with your parents as an adult or when they move in with you, it's essential to address questions related to living arrangements, rules, and responsibilities up front (or as upfront as possible). Discussing financial contributions, the duration of cohabitation (how long is this arrangement in effect? Short-term? Long-term? In-definitely?), as well as any privacy needs in advance can prevent potential conflicts and ensure more comfortable living situations. Open communication fosters trust and strengthens your relationship and being open and honest about your needs is essential.

Additionally, the chapter emphasizes the importance of giving your parents the benefit of the doubt during misunderstandings. Recognizing that most people are generally doing their best and understanding that they may not have the same tools or resources as you is crucial. We have to realize that our parents are not us, and we are not our parents. It is very possible that they have no idea that they're hurting you or upsetting you. It is vital that you discuss with them what you feel is appropriate and open that dialogue up.

Always be respectful in your communication with your parents. Avoid using offensive language, or language they deem offensive whenever possible.

Lastly, the chapter emphasizes the need for "you" time. Prioritizing self-care will give you time to relax and recharge. Exercising, hobbies, meditation, writing, etc. are all great practices for self-care. Remember, "you" time is about doing activities that bring you joy, peace, and personal fulfillment. It's a time to recharge and reconnect with yourself, so that you can give others what they need from you, too.

Chapter Seven

Socializing with your Parents as an Adult

In this chapter, we delve into the art of maintaining a rich and rewarding relationship with your parents as an adult. Communication is different as you transition, so therefore, being social with them is also different. This is a time when you and your parents can finally be on some equal footing and grow your relationship beyond that of a parent-child relationship. It's a time to get to know them for them and maintain the bond you'll have for the rest of your lives.

Call Them Often

Regular communication is the cornerstone of any healthy relationship. In the hustle and bustle of adult life, it's easy to lose touch with the people who matter most. To bridge the gap, pick up the phone and call your parents as regularly as you can; and when you can't, text them. A simple "how are you?" can really do wonders; and an even more in-depth conversation about your lives can strengthen and maintain the bond you have with your family. Frequent communication is an expression of your love and care. It assures your parents that they are an important part of your life and that you value them and choose them as a priority.

Bear in mind, keeping in touch is not only about sharing your own experiences but about staying updated on theirs. Hearing about their daily activities, their future goals, their achievements, and struggles creates a deeper understanding of them as people. It also gives you a chance to empathize with them and truly walk in their shoes. Because ultimately, our parents likely didn't tell us everything while we were kids—but now you have a chance to truly engage with them with equal footing which can strengthen the bond you have with them. Conversations over the phone can be as comforting as a warm hug, creating a sense of closeness even when physical distances separate you.

Just the act of reaching out shows them that you're being proactive and choosing them. In turn that can make it easier for them to initiate contact in the future.

Let Them Confide in You

Your parents have played the roles of protectors, mentors, and confidants for most of your life. As you mature into adulthood, you have the opportunity to return the favor. Create a space where your parents feel safe to confide in you, sharing their thoughts, joys, and concerns. Your role as a caring and attentive listener can offer them much-needed emotional support. Be their friend; be their family; be their shoulder to lean on if they want you to be.

Allowing your parents to open up to you is not just a one-sided exchange, it's a mutually beneficial process. Their ability to share their experiences, feelings, and wisdom provides you with an opportunity to learn and grow. By encouraging their confidences, you create a deeper level of intimacy, respect, and understanding in your relationship. This can foster a sense of mutual trust and reinforce the idea that you're there for each other, no matter the circumstances. Just like we have always been taught family is all about.

As your parents confide in you, be sure to exercise patience and empathy just like you'd expect them to give you if the roles were reversed (which, by now, I'm sure it has been reversed many times). Even if their concerns might seem trivial or irrelevant at the moment, remember that their emotions are real and significant and there were probably times that your issues seemed trivial. By offering a listening ear and a shoulder to lean on, you're giving them a valuable gift: the assurance that their thoughts and feelings matter.

Hug Your Parents When You See Them

Physical touch is a universal language of affection and a way to express emotions and convey love and appreciation. In fact, one of the simplest yet most profound ways to convey your feelings is by giving your parents a warm, heartfelt hug as soon as you see them.

Hugs are not just gestures of greeting; they can be symbols of love, acceptance, and reassurance. When you embrace your parents, you're telling them that you're grateful for them, their presence, and that you cherish the time you have together and that you're genuinely pleased to see them. These sentiments can go a long way.

The act of hugging can also release oxytocin, which is similar to endorphins and serotonin and commonly referred to as the "love hormone". It has the power to reduce stress and anxiety, lower blood pressure, and create a sense of emotional connection. In this way, hugging your parents not only communicates love and appreciation but also brings about physiological benefits, reinforcing the importance of physical contact in maintaining a strong bond.

Get Together for the Holidays

Holidays offer the perfect occasion for family reunions and the opportunity to celebrate the bond you share with your parents. Whether it's the traditional holidays such as Thanksgiving, Christmas, or New Year's, or more unique family celebrations, coming together during these special moments strengthens your familial ties.

Sometimes as families age, people can start to move away or drift apart. It may be difficult as the family tree branches out to get together on the bigger holidays. However, by creating or even just revamping your family traditions and rituals, you can figure out ways to get together. In fact, even making this a project with your parents can be a unique way to bond with them. For instance, you might establish an annual family picnic or a "family day" where you engage in various activities together. These don't have to be near or on big holidays. Many families choose to do these sorts of events on nice, warm weather days that can get the kids outside playing and give the adults a chance to soak in some Vitamin D and enjoy time together. This may be difficult to plan—weather-wise—if you'd like it to be on the same day annually. But choose a time when the weather is generally mild and have indoor and outdoor activities in mind! These traditions build a sense of togetherness and make your relationship with your entire family feel more special and distinctive.

Additionally, just taking the time to prepare and enjoy meals together during the holidays or your family events can be a deep bonding experience. Cooking together, sharing recipes, and savoring all of the dishes you've prepared together can create cherished memories for many years to come.

Let Them Spend Time with Your Kids

If you have children of your own, involve your parents in their lives. Allowing your parents to spend quality time with their grandchildren can be an enriching experience for both generations. It allows your children to experience familial bonds but also gives them a different perspective. After all, you and your parents are different people and come from different generations. They may help your children grow into more well-rounded youngsters as they experience more and socialize with people from different walks of life.

Giving your parents a chance to be with their grandchildren offers a truly unique relationship. Your parents get to be grandparents (which is always a bit different than being parents) and your children get to benefit from their wisdom and unconditional love. Grandparents often bring a different perspective and approach to child-rearing.

Moreover, involving your parents in your children's lives can be a way to reciprocate their efforts and sacrifices in raising you. It allows them to witness and participate in the joys and milestones of the next generation.

Treat Them

Occasionally, surprise your parents with small treats or tokens of appreciation. Whether it's a favorite homemade meal, a thoughtful gift, or a special outing, these gestures show that you value and cherish your relationship with them. These acts of kindness can create moments of fun and joy and also reinforce the love you share for one another.

Consider taking them out for ice cream now and then, or go to a movie—and *you* pick up the bill. Make it an entire family affair for even more fun and make sure you show them that you're happy they're there with you (especially if you have your own family now).

Experience New Activities or Hobbies Together

As adults, we all have hobbies; and there may be some that you already enjoy participating in with your parents. However, exploring brand new activities or hobbies together with your parents can be an exciting way to bond. It creates memories and you begin to associate this fun and new experience with your parent(s) which can truly strengthen your relationship.

Whether it's learning a new skill, embarking on a creative project together, or engaging in a shared interest that neither of you has tried before, it can really improve your connection with them. Some hobbies you might consider are:

- **Cooking or Baking:** Experimenting with new recipes or baking homemade treats that you saw online or on TV can be fun and delicious.

- **Gardening:** Gardening is not only a relaxing hobby but can also lead to beautiful results.

- **Painting or Drawing:** Explore your artistic side by taking up painting, drawing, or other forms of visual art. You can create your own art or attend art classes. Now there are even "painting with a twist" classes that involve wine and other fun elements.

- **Hiking or Nature Walks:** Enjoy the great outdoors by going on hikes or nature walks in local parks or nature reserves. It's an excellent way to stay active and appreciate nature.

- **Photography:** Capture moments and memories by taking up photography. You can explore your surroundings and document your adventures together.

- **Playing Musical Instruments:** Learning a new instrument together can be difficult, but also incredibly rewarding! Consider taking joint classes and jamming together.

- **Birdwatching:** Birdwatching can be a relaxing and educational hobby. Get a pair of binoculars and observe the various bird species in your area. Put up a few feeders nearby and enjoy them up close, as well.

- **Knitting:** Learning how to make your own garments or blankets can be fun and can give you and your parents a chance to catch up and talk while you make them!

- **Wine or Beer Tasting:** If you're of legal drinking age and appreciate beer or wine, you can explore different wineries or breweries together.

- **Puzzle Solving:** Work on jigsaw puzzles, crosswords, or brain-teasers together. Puzzle-solving can be a mentally stimulating and enjoyable pastime. There are subscription boxes you can sign up for, too, so make it a monthly ritual to solve a new one together!

- **Dancing:** Learn different dance styles such as ballroom, salsa, or swing dancing. You can take classes or learn from YouTube.

- **Book Club:** Start a family book club and read and discuss books together. It's an excellent way to share your thoughts and insights on various literature—and this can even open up the door to more in-depth and meaningful discussions.

- **Yoga or Meditation:** We discussed that self-care is important, and yoga and meditation is a great two-for-one. You can practice self-care and participate in great quality time with your parent if you do it together! Use it as a way to stay healthy and reduce stress and if you want to make it extra fun, attend a class together.

- **Volunteer Work:** Find a cause or organization each of you are passionate about and sign up to volunteer. It's a meaningful way to give back to the community together as a family.

- **Stargazing:** Bring the chairs and the snacks and spend evenings stargazing and identifying constellations. Consider investing in a telescope for a more in-depth celestial exploration and keep track of events happening in your viewing area.

- **Model Car Building:** Pick up an old craft such as building model cars! It's possible this can hold some nostalgia behind it, but if either of you are car fans, definitely consider this as a fun, engaging, and satisfying option.

- **Home Improvement:** Collaborate on home improvement projects or DIY renovations. This can be a productive and satisfying way to upgrade your living space. Branch out, too, and potentially earn extra cash in the meantime.

- **Travel:** Plan and take trips together. Make sure you're exploring new places, cultures, and cuisines since this is all about trying new things together and truly experiencing things with one another. Traveling can create unforgettable shared experiences.

Remember that the key to a successful shared hobby is to choose activities that all parties can enjoy and that align with everyone's interests and abilities; but really make sure that whatever you and your family choose, you're able to experience it for the first time, together, and that you stay consistent and keep at it!

Take Them on Family Vacations

Introducing your parents to travel can be an incredibly rewarding and enriching experience. It's a chance to create cherished memories across the globe and discover completely unchartered territory together. This not only strengthens your familial bond but helps you all grow individually in your own personal journey. Traveling abroad may take careful planning, but it is an opportunity to open the door to other cultures or ideals that you may not experience on the regular. When you plan a trip internationally, it is important to ensure that everyone has a fulfilling and enjoyable experience. It is important that we take essential steps and strategies for a fun time for everyone. This is everything from choosing the right destination to striking the perfect balance between new experiences and comfortable ones.

Choose Locations Carefully

Getting your folks on board is often as simple as finding out where they want to go. However, it's not always as easy as asking them, especially if they're the type to go with the flow or the type that wants to eagerly please everyone. If they are like that, it may be up to you to come up with something, and in order to do that, think about what they might enjoy. Maybe they're history buffs with a special interest in World War II? Maybe they love going to the theater together? Or maybe their ancestors came from another country that they might like to visit? Have they ever mentioned something like an African safari or seeing Egyptian pyramids? Try to find some interests and go from there!

Pick an "Easier" Location if They're Not Used to Traveling

Baby steps are usually a good idea for novice travelers of any age. A DIY trip through India, for instance, might be a more challenging adventure for many travelers and it may be better to start small.

Instead, opt for a place without a language barrier, and, for those who aren't quite as adventurous, potentially look at places with familiar foods. When there are fewer things to worry about regarding pushing your parents out of their comfort zone, the more likely they may be to try something new along the way. Cruises can be a good option because they cater to a multitude of different people at any given time. Also, your parents can enjoy excursions and adventure during the day, and then come back to the familiarity of the ship afterward. This option can also help when dealing with finances because a majority of the expenses are paid beforehand.

Start Slow

As stated, baby steps can be useful. Although you may not think it's worth the long flight for a trip that's shorter than two weeks, for your parents' first international trip you should probably start with something shorter. A 5–7-day trip in one place with a day trip or two may be a better option unless your parents are particularly adventurous. Think of it like the sampler platter at a new restaurant you go to—they'll get to try a few things so that they know better what suits them for the next time. This is great because it prevents them from being completely overwhelmed by too much all at once.

Figure Out Budget and Finances Ahead of Time

Are you fronting the entire bill for this? If not, it's definitely worth talking about beforehand. As awkward as discussions about money can be with your family, they're still necessary to have before a big trip. If you want to treat them to an international trip, that's wonderful—but if you're not paying for everything, it's critical to make sure they know that and to ensure that they can afford the trip. Decide before you book anything who is paying for what!

Don't Over-schedule Your Days

Even if you don't think you're a fast-paced traveler, chances are good that you'd pack more into a day than your parents might. Travel can be overwhelming and incredibly exhausting, even when it's great. Remember that everyone benefits from being well-rested. No one wants to vacation with someone that's grouchy because they're tired or hungry!

If you're touring a museum or doing something strenuous in the morning, leave the afternoon open. If you've got plans to have a late dinner and see a show, allow for sleeping in or naps (or both) earlier in the day. Make sure everyone is well-fed and well-rested.

It's also important to note any mobility issues your parents may have. Even if they're still spry, spending a whole day walking on cobblestone streets can be hard on joints. Consider their regular schedule at home—and how much more active you'll all be when traveling—and plan accordingly.

Get Everyone Involved in the Planning Stage

This is the one time that you can't just let someone say, "Whatever you want to do is fine!". Make sure everyone going on your trip has input and talks about what they want to do! Top priorities need to be included in the itinerary.

No matter what you have to do to get the feedback, make sure that you do. Even if you have to instigate every planning session. Even if you have to send them links to articles or drop off guidebooks for them. Make sure they look, research, and let you know anything they'd like to do. This alleviates surprises during the trip and also makes everyone feel represented!

Plan as much as Possible in Advance

Whether or not you're the type of traveler who plans ahead, it's an important thing to keep in mind when taking your parents abroad for the first time.

It will mean less wasted time during the trip going back and forth on the topic of what to do every day. It means booking skip-the-line tours, so no one has to stand for hours outside any given attraction. It means everyone knows (and approves of) the itinerary in advance and isn't surprised last minute with something they don't want to do.

Balance New Experiences with Comfortable Ones

For many of us, learning and experiencing new things is one of the biggest perks of traveling. That doesn't have to change when you bring your parents along for the ride, even if they're a bit less adventurous than you are. It is likely that you have a good sense of where your parents' comfort zones are and what might be pushing it too far. Find ways to make sure they're not spending too much time being uncomfortable. This can be achieved by proper balance. Go out to eat that adventurous meal for lunch but opt for a more familiar dinner. And on the flip side, if they're more adventurous than you are, be open to trying things but make sure they opt for something a little more mild afterward. You never know, they may push you to do something you might not have done otherwise. Balance makes sure that all of you are happy!

Plan Some Alone Time

This may sound counter-intuitive to going on a vacation with your parents, but it is a good idea to carve out a little alone time—especially if you're also going with your partner. See if they wouldn't mind doing one activity while you and your spouse do another. Or maybe you guys want to hang back while they go to that museum down the street. Either way, just plan out one or two things during the trip that you can do on your own (or with your partner).

This is particularly important if you live a bit further away from your parents and haven't spent a lot of time with them in recent years. Even during a week-long trip, you may want to plan a day in the middle where you all get a break from one another. After all, everyone needs a chance to reset their clock. This is especially true if there are CDs in the mix.

Keep Everyone in Mind

This may be the most important—and most difficult—thing to keep in mind. You worked hard for those vacation days and saved up to go on this trip, and the last thing you want is to come home disappointed. When you decide to introduce international travel to your folks, you're signing on to take them on a trip that suits them as well. Depending on your parents, that might mean hotels instead of hostels, taxis instead of walking, museums instead of nightclubs, and more sit-down restaurants than street food. The perfect trip is out there, for both you and your parents. And you never know, they may just surprise you with how much adventure they're willing to have!

Plan Family Game Nights

When you sit down to play a game with your family, you are building relationships, making space for important conversations, practicing all-important social skills, working on brain and strategy skills, and probably most importantly—you're making memories.

If game nights have always been a part of your family's culture, it may not seem like that hundredth run of Monopoly is important, but it is. You are building something larger, something that you can't see right now, but something that is vitally important! So, play, enjoy each other, and make memories!

Schedule a Time that Works for Everyone

The term "family game night" means the family is involved, but it doesn't have to mean playing into the night. Schedule a time that works best for you and your family. Whenever there's downtime, you should schedule your family games. Just make sure you set a day and a time that works for all members of your family and then try to stick to it. Consistency will mean the most in this. If a weekly game night is too overwhelming, try something monthly first! It's not supposed to feel like a chore, but it should require a bit of sacrifice. It doesn't matter when or how often, it's just that you pick something that can work so you can stick to it.

Pick More Than One Game

Have a few games in mind for any given night. Some families may have favorites they want to play every time, while others may want to keep a rotation of a few tried and true. But keep it fun and fresh with a few curveballs from time to time. And then there are families that may prefer a new game every single time. Consider rotating who picks the game or brings it; or possibly set up on a subscription that sends new games every month. Whatever you decide, make sure everyone is on board and it's something that is appropriate and easy enough for everyone intended to play to play!

Do Not Disturb

Set your phone to Do Not Disturb mode. Having technology at your fingertips is wonderful, but you don't need it for game night. That is, unless you choose to incorporate video games. Turn off televisions and other distractions as well. This is a time for family!

Make Sure There's Food

Everyone loves food; everyone loves drinks. Make sure that you have plenty planned, whether it's takeout or something you cook, or even take turns providing between you and your family members. Every time there's a game night planned, make sure food is involved.

Remember To Have Fun

It's easy to get wrapped up in everyday life. It's even easier to let it affect your mood when you spend time with your family. But don't let it! This is a time for you and yours, so enjoy each other and remember that real life will be there when you're finished with your time together. Game nights should be fun and stress-free, even if the game itself is new and challenging. Try to relax, be mindful of the moment, and know that you're creating memories that can last a lifetime!

Be Patient

If you're the type to be overly competitive, make sure you're being patient with those who may need a bit more time to understand the game. Be patient with children who may argue and just explain to them calmly that it's a game and that you're all learning and trying to have fun together. Understand that all game nights won't be perfect and don't let your expectations ruin the good nature of the evening. Kids will argue. Tears may even happen to our more sensitive family members. Accusations of cheating may flow. There may also be sore winners and sore losers. Whatever the case, just remember that you and your family are together and you're playing. And use these times as teachable moments for you and your family to discuss the many ways to improve.

Thank Everyone for Coming

This may sound silly, but when everyone is finished playing, thank them. Thank them for coming, thank them for playing, and thank them for interacting with one another. Tell them you had fun playing with them and that you're looking forward to the next night.

Plan the Next One

Even if you have the same day and time in place for every game night, make sure you plan the next one. This can be as simple as confirming everyone will be there on the day and time agreed upon. You can also ask what you're having for dinner that night. Just make sure that you plan it and that everyone has it locked into their calendars, so they don't forget.

Revisit Places of Significance

Revisiting places that are important to you is often an emotional experience, but revisiting a place that is important to both you and your parents is at times some of the best medicine you can give to your relationship. Revisiting places that hold special meaning for all of you can oftentimes rekindle fond memories. Going back to places where you've shared significant moments can evoke nostalgia and remind you of the journey you've all taken together. It may even remind you why love your parents so much in the first place.

These places are part of your shared life together and revisiting them reinforces the idea that you've all built something meaningful over time and are a true family unit. Reliving positive experiences can be beneficial to all of you and your respective mental health. Make the most out of revisiting by:

- Planning Together: Discuss which places hold the most meaning for each of you. It could be the place where your parents first met or fell in love; a place where you had your first family vacation or getaway; your childhood town; a baseball field you grew up going to; anything that holds significance to you.

- Scheduling Visits: Make plans to visit these kinds of places periodically. You can schedule a day trip or weekend getaway to spend quality time there. Definitely consider making these sorts of revisits part of an anniversary tradition or ritual.

- Creating New Memories: Don't always rely on your nostalgia to get you through. When you go back to this special place, make sure that you're trying to create new memories together there.

- Share Reflections: Talk about your feelings and memories associated with these places. This is a great bonding exercise.

- Stay Present: While revisiting, stay present in the moment. Put away your cell phone and focus only on each other.

Key Takeaways

In this chapter, we've explored essential strategies and activities to maintain a strong and fulfilling relationship with your parents as an adult and how you might socialize with them now that you're grown!

First thing is first—communicate! Make it a habit to call your parents regularly. Frequent conversations bridge any kind of distance gaps between you and reassure them of your love and appreciation. Be proactive in reaching out. Don't always wait for them to make the first move. This will demonstrate your commitment to maintaining a relationship with them.

During your discussions, encourage your parents to confide in you and share their thoughts and feelings. Don't let your relationship be one-sided. This is supposed to be something that evolves over time rather than stays stagnant. Be sure to improve upon and nurture your existing relationship. By asking them how they are, or to confide in you, you show that you are offering emotional support and are trying to understand them more. Be patient and empathetic as you listen.

When you can see your parents, do. Make sure you're spending holidays together or at the very least special occasions. Prepare meals with one another, give gifts—celebrate however you like—but make sure you're building memories. While you're with them, remember that physical touch, such as hugging your parents when you see them, is also extremely important as it helps to convey deep emotions you have for them and strengthens your bond. After all, hugs are symbols of love, acceptance, and reassurance, and they also have physiological and psychological benefits.

If you have children, make sure you're letting your parents be involved in their lives. The bond between grandparent and grandchild can be incredibly special and lend a unique perspective to their upbringing. The difference in generation can give your child a great perspective and teach them how different their lives are from your parents' upbringing. Allowing this opportunity to connect can potentially show your child the beauty of empathy and relating to others.

Another important aspect we dug into in this chapter was the importance of treating your parents from time to time! It's likely that they treated you your entire childhood. Use your adulthood to return the favor, including potentially taking them on trips with you. You don't have to pay for their entire trip, especially if you don't have the money, but maybe invite them and treat them to one or two things along the way.

Finally, make sure that you're exploring new activities and hobbies with them and spending quality time such as family game nights with them. These sorts of interactive activities can enhance your connection together and create unique memories you wouldn't have had otherwise.

Chapter Eight

Final Thoughts

As we come to the final chapter in this journey to provide 50 Ways to Love Your Parents, it's essential to reflect on the path we've traveled, exploring the intricate dance of love with its different personality types—the Cave Dweller (CD), the Mountain Yeller (MY), and the Straddler, who possesses elements of both. Throughout this book, we have delved into the significance of understanding these personality types, how to communicate effectively, growing a bond into adulthood with our parents, and cultivating that bond for years to come.

Love truly is a dynamic and evolving force that connects us in ways we can never truly predict. Your parents are human beings, and those human beings are complex and beautiful.

Formulating and fostering a successful relationship is not about finding the perfect formula or mastering a set of guidelines. Instead, it's about the dedication and effort we put into nurturing the unique bonds we have with our parents. Your parents (whether they're a CD or an MY or somewhere in between) will appreciate the steps you have taken to communicate with and understand them in a way that creates a lasting relationship. They will appreciate you making them a priority.

The Importance of Continuous Effort and Growth in Relationships

Our journey together in this book has underscored the importance of continuous effort and growth in relationships. Love is not a static concept but instead is a force that thrives on the energy we invest in it. Every day, we have the opportunity to learn, adapt, and grow in our relationships. Our personalities evolve, and our needs change. It is forever important that we communicate with one another, focus on ourselves and our significant others and continue to maintain self-growth as well as growth within our relationships in order to be our happiest selves.

Embracing the Nature of Love and Understanding

Love is not a one-size-fits-all concept. It is as diverse and complex as the human beings who experience it. Through the pages of this book, we've explored the three fundamental personality types in great detail. The fact that each personality type or individual may demonstrate their love differently shows that there is no right or wrong way to love. It is important we celebrate these differences and embrace the individuality of each and every person and relationship.

Learning Through Differences

The differences between personality types and individuals absolutely creates opportunities to truly develop patience, understanding, and empathy, especially when we focus on each other's individual emotional strengths. In learning fifty ways to love your parents, you have expanded your horizon and broadened your perspective—and hopefully given you the tools and resources needed to learn from your parents and the love they share with you. Embrace the differences you share and their different emotional strengths. Learn from them and enhance your own emotional strengths.

Cherish Your Love

As we conclude this book, it is important for you to leave you with the encouragement to continually evolve, adapt, and cherish the love you have for your parents. Use the knowledge and insights gained from this guide as tools for strengthening the bond you have with them.

It is quite easy to begin to take someone for granted, especially after growing comfortable with them or when you find yourself moving in an opposing direction for one reason or another. Over time it is natural to stop saying "thank you" as often, or to stop appreciating things they do for you. This leads to eventually devaluing one another, and this leads to no longer cherishing one another.

Never stop cherishing them because we only have a finite amount of time on this earth. If you can, pretend every day is a new day to find a way to show your appreciation and imprint on their lives. Use the guidelines of this book to understand their needs and desires and how to continue to make them smile as often as possible.

Stay Curious

Curiosity doesn't kill the cat. It keeps the cat interesting, and it keeps the world around it interesting. Stay curious about yourself, stay curious about the people you love, and you will never become bored or stop trying to make time for them.

Start with yourself. Never stop learning about and working on yourself. It's often easy to focus on others' shortcomings and overlook your own personal struggles. Hopefully, as you have learned more about your own motivations, areas of strength and struggle, as well as any unmet desires or needs that you may have, you have developed a new curiosity to discover more as well as improve on any shortcomings you may have.

When you place your parents on equal footing to yourself and realize that they're people too, you begin to realize it is quite natural to have shortcomings. However, reflecting on this book, it is also a joy to realize that they also have strengths in areas that you may not have realized before, and you can now look forward to finding out more about them. See yourself; see your family. Explore one another and meet in a moment of mutual discovery to grow closer and create a stronger bond with one another. Since none of you should ever stop growing, there should always be something new to discover about one another during your many family moments.

Make Time

Of course, being curious and discovering more about one another will take quite a bit of time and investment into your relationship. So, take the time! There will be inconsistency as you all continue your journey through this life. This happens for a lot of different reasons, but mostly it happens as you transition into new seasons of life. These are times of so much chaos and so much change that it is easy to feel spread thin as it is. Prioritizing your relationship with your family is vital. This is why your regular check-ins are so important. Ask one another, "Are we making enough time?" It may seem obvious, but that small gesture will open you all up to being honest about whether you feel properly invested.

There are times that you need time to talk about the nitty-gritty or the "business" of your family, but there will also be times that one of you just needs time to vent or needs emotional support. In those moments, all of you need to understand something: togetherness is what matters. Remember, you are going through this life with each other. Make the time with them to ensure that it's a fun, compassionate, healthy, and emotionally fulfilling life. Moments of laughter and silliness or shared activity can bring such a bond of closeness at the end of each and every day. So always make the time. No matter if they are a CD, an MY, or somewhere in between, they, like you, crave that precious quality time together. Love, at its core, is all about being present in the moments you share. Make the time, cherish each other, and embrace the ever-evolving journey of love.

Appendices

Self-Assessment Questionnaire: Determine If You're a CD, MY, or Straddler

In the quest for self-understanding, recognizing one's intrinsic personality traits plays a crucial role. This self-assessment questionnaire has been carefully designed to help you discern whether you align most closely with the introspective nature of a Cave Dweller (CD), the extroverted inclinations of a Mountain Yeller (MY), or the balanced characteristics of a Straddler. By reflecting on your behaviors, preferences, and reactions in various situations, this tool aims to provide insight into your predominant personality type. Approach each question with honesty and openness, and remember, there's no right or wrong answer—just a deeper understanding of your unique self waiting to be unveiled.

Personality Indicator #1

Circle one answer per question.

1. Have you ever walked in your sleep during your adult life?

    YES or NO

2. As a teenager, did you feel comfortable expressing your feelings to one or both of your parents?

    YES or NO

3. Do you have a tendency to look directly into a person's eyes when talking to them?

    YES or NO

4. Do you feel that most people, when you first meet them, are uncritical of your appearance?

    YES or NO

5. In a group situation with people you've just met, would you feel comfortable drawing attention to yourself by initiating a conversation?

    YES or NO

6. Do you feel comfortable holding hands or hugging someone you're in a relationship with in front of other people?

    YES or NO

7. When someone talks about feeling warm physically, do you begin to feel warm also?

   YES or NO

8. Do you tend to tune out when someone is talking to you because you're anxious to come up with your side of the story?

   YES or NO

9. Do you feel that you learn better by seeing and/or reading than by hearing?

   YES or NO

10. In a new class or company meeting, do you usually feel comfortable asking questions in front of the group?

    YES or NO

11. When expressing your ideas, do you find it important to relate all the details leading up to the subject so the other person can understand it completely?

    YES or NO

12. Do you enjoy relating to children?

    YES or NO

13. Are you comfortable with your body movements when faced with unfamiliar people and circumstances?

YES or NO

14. Do you prefer reading fiction rather than nonfiction?

YES or NO

15. If you were to imagine sucking on a juicy lemon, would your mouth water?

YES or NO

16. Do you feel comfortable receiving a compliment in front of other people?

YES or NO

17. Do you feel that you're a good conversationalist?

YES or NO

18. Do you feel comfortable when complimentary attention is drawn to your physical body?

YES or NO

Personality Indicator #2

Circle one answer per question.

1. Have you ever awakened in the middle of the night and felt that you could not move your body and/or talk?

YES or NO

50 WAYS TO LOVE YOUR PARENTS

2. As a child, did you feel you were more affected by your parents' tone of voice than by what they actually said?

YES or NO

3. If someone you know talks about a fear that you've experienced before, do you have a tendency to re-experience that apprehension or fear?

YES or NO

4. After having an argument with someone, do you tend to dwell on what you could or should have said?

YES or NO

5. Do you tend to occasionally tune out when someone is talking to you and, therefore, don't hear what's being said because your mind drifts to something totally unrelated?

YES or NO

6. Do you sometimes desire to be complimented for a job well done but feel embarrassed or uncomfortable when complemented?

YES or NO

7. Do you often fear not being able to carry on a conversation with someone you've just met?

YES or NO

8. Do you feel self-conscious when attention is drawn to your

physical body or appearance?

YES or NO

9. If you had a choice, would you rather avoid being around children most of the time?

YES or NO

10. Do you feel uptight in body movements, especially when faced with unfamiliar people or circumstances?

YES or NO

11. Do you prefer reading nonfiction rather than fiction?

YES or NO

12. If someone describes a very bitter taste, do you have difficulty experiencing the physical feeling of that bitter taste?

YES or NO

13. Do you generally feel that you see yourself less favorably than others see you?

YES or NO

14. Do you tend to feel awkward or self-conscious holding hands and/or kissing someone you're in a relationship with in front of other people?

YES or NO

15. In a new lecture or company meeting, do you usually feel uncomfortable asking questions in front of the group?

    YES or NO

16. Do you feel uneasy if someone you've just met looks you directly in the eyes when talking to you, especially if the conversation is about you?

    YES or NO

17. In a group situation with people you've just met, would you feel uncomfortable drawing attention to yourself by initiating a conversation?

    YES or NO

18. If you're in a relationship or are very close to someone, do you find it difficult or embarrassing to verbalize your love for them?

    YES or NO

Personality Indicator Scores

Personality Indicator #1

- Give yourself 10 points for every "yes" answer for questions 1 and 2.

- Give yourself 5 points for every answer for questions 3–18.

- Write the total number at the top of the #1 questionnaire.

Personality Indicator #2

- Give yourself 10 points for every yes answer for questions 1 and 2.

- Give yourself 5 points for every answer for questions 3–18.

- Write the total number at the top of the #2 questionnaire.

- Combine the total from Personality Indicators 1 and 2.

Using the Scoring Chart

On the scoring chart, look up the combined score of Personality Indicator 1 and 2 on the HORIZONTAL axis of the chart and circle the number.

- Take the total score of Personality Indicator #1, locate it on the VERTICAL axis of the chart, and circle the number.

- Draw a horizontal line across the page from the Personality Indicator 1 score, then draw a vertical line down from the combined score.

- The number in the box where the two lines intersect represents your true, adjusted percentage Personality Indicator.

- Scores 61 and higher indicate a Mountain Yeller personality type.

- Scores 45 and lower indicate a Cave Dweller personality type.

- Scores 47–56 indicate a Straddler personality type.

Cave Dweller Tendencies

- Reserved
- Head ruled
- Controlling
- Wants space and security
- Prefers socializing one-on-one
- Singular focus
- Thinks before reacting
- Prefers showing affection privately
- Distrusts flattery
- Enjoys working alone
- Enjoys individual activities
- Wants alone time
- Dresses for comfort
- Decides after thinking about it
- Speaks literally—to the point
- Infers from what others say
- Feels emotional pain in the mind
- Fears loss of security

Cave Dweller Priorities

- Career/Financial Security
- Hobbies/Children
- Relationships/Family
- Sex/Lovers

Mountain Yeller Tendencies

- Outgoing
- Heart ruled
- Dominating
- Wants connection and touch
- Enjoys socializing in groups
- Moving focus
- Reacts spontaneously
- Comfortable with affection anytime
- Likes reassurance and compliments
- Enjoys working with people
- Enjoys team activities
- Wants to be together as much as possible

- Decides in the moment
- Speaks inferentially—adds story
- Takes literally what others say
- Feels emotional pain in body and mind
- Fears rejection

Mountain Yeller Priorities

- Relationships/Sex
- Family/Children
- Friends/Hobbies
- Career/Financial security

SCORE # 1 / COMBINED SCORE #1 AND #2

0	5	10	15	20	25	30	35	40	45	50	55	60	65	70	75	80	85	90	95	100	Combined
0	10	20	30	40	50	60	70	80	90	100											50
0	9	18	27	36	45	55	64	73	82	91	100										55
0	8	17	25	33	42	50	58	67	75	83	92	100									60
0	8	15	23	31	38	46	54	62	69	77	85	92	100								65
0	7	14	21	29	36	43	50	57	64	71	79	86	93	100							70
0	7	13	20	27	33	40	47	53	60	67	73	80	87	93	100						75
0	6	13	19	25	31	38	44	50	56	63	69	75	81	88	94	100					80
0	6	12	18	24	29	35	41	47	53	59	65	71	76	82	88	94	100				85
0	6	11	17	22	28	33	39	44	50	56	61	67	72	78	83	89	94	100			90
0	5	11	16	21	26	32	37	42	47	53	58	63	68	74	79	84	89	95	100		95
0	5	10	15	20	25	30	35	40	45	50	55	60	65	70	75	80	85	90	95	100	100
0	5	10	14	19	24	29	33	38	43	48	52	57	62	67	71	76	81	86	90	95	105
0	5	9	14	18	23	27	32	36	41	45	50	55	59	64	68	73	77	82	86	91	110
0	4	9	13	17	22	26	30	35	39	43	48	52	57	61	65	70	74	78	83	87	115
0	4	8	13	17	21	25	29	33	38	42	46	50	54	58	63	67	71	75	79	83	120
0	4	8	12	16	20	24	28	32	36	40	44	48	52	56	60	64	68	72	76	80	125
0	4	8	12	15	19	23	27	31	35	38	42	46	50	54	58	62	65	69	73	77	130
0	4	7	11	15	19	22	26	30	33	37	41	44	48	52	56	59	63	67	70	74	135
0	4	7	11	14	18	21	25	29	32	36	39	43	46	50	54	57	61	64	68	71	140
0	3	7	10	14	17	21	24	28	31	34	38	41	45	48	52	55	59	62	66	69	145
0	3	7	10	13	17	20	23	27	30	33	37	40	43	47	50	53	57	60	63	67	150
0	3	6	10	13	16	19	23	26	29	32	35	39	42	45	48	52	55	58	61	65	155
0	3	6	9	13	16	19	22	25	28	31	34	38	41	44	47	50	53	56	59	63	160
0	3	6	9	12	15	18	21	24	27	30	33	36	39	42	45	48	52	55	58	61	165
0	3	6	9	12	15	18	21	24	26	29	32	35	38	41	44	47	50	53	56	59	170
0	3	6	9	11	14	17	20	23	26	29	31	34	37	40	43	46	49	51	54	57	175
0	3	6	8	11	14	17	19	22	25	28	31	33	36	39	42	44	47	50	53	56	180
0	3	5	8	11	14	16	19	22	24	27	30	32	35	38	41	43	46	49	51	54	185
0	3	5	8	11	13	16	18	21	24	26	29	32	34	37	39	42	45	47	50	53	190
0	3	5	8	10	13	15	18	21	23	26	28	31	33	36	38	41	44	46	49	51	195
0	3	5	8	10	13	15	18	20	23	25	28	30	33	35	38	40	43	45	48	50	200

About the Author

Dr. Cline lives with her husband, two daughters, two German Shepherds, and two Yorkies in the hills of North Carolina. Her expertise in relationship building has offered her the opportunity to travel around the world as a keynote speaker and international workshop facilitator.

www.ingramcontent.com/pod-product-compliance
Lightning Source LLC
Chambersburg PA
CBHW070110080526
44586CB00013B/1253